THE DECISION-MAKER'S
GUIDE TO
401(k) PLANS

THE DECISION-MAKER'S GUIDE TO

401(k)

PLANS

How to set up cost-effective plans in companies of all sizes

Stephen J. Butler

Berrett-Koehler Publishers
San Francisco

Berrett-Koehler Publishers, Inc.
155 Montgomery Street
San Francisco, CA 94104-4109
Tel: 415-288-0260 Fax: 415-362-2512

Ordering Information

Individual sales. Berrett-Koehler publications are available through most bookstores. They can also be ordered direct from Berrett-Koehler at the address above.

Quantity sales. Special discounts are available on quantity purchases by corporations, associations, and others. For details, contact the "Special Sales Department" at the Berrett-Koehler address above.

Orders for college textbook/course adoption use. Please contact Berrett-Koehler Publishers at the address above.

Orders by U.S. trade bookstores and wholesalers. Please contact Publishers Group West, 4065 Hollis Street, Box 8843, Emeryville, CA 94662; 510-658-3453; 1-800-788-3123.

Printed in the United States of America

Printed on acid-free and recycled paper (50 percent recycled fiber, including 10 percent postconsumer waste).

Library of Congress Cataloging-in-Publication Data
Butler, Stephen J., 1944–
  The decision-maker's guide to 401(k) plans : how to set up cost-
effective plans in companies of all sizes / by Stephen J. Butler.
   p. cm.
  ISBN 1–881052–64–8
  1. 401(k) plans. I. Title
HF5549.5.C67B89 1995   95–4178
658.3'253—dc20   CIP

First Edition

99 98 97 96 95   10 9 8 7 6 5 4 3 2 1

To my wife, Frances Knox Butler

Table of Contents

Preface

Today, company owners and senior managers (those people I call decision-makers) receive most of their information regarding 401(k) plans from someone trying to sell them the services that these plans require. Consequently, this information may not be as objective as it could be.

The purpose of this book is to "tell it like it is" and to debunk a few myths in the process. The net effect, I hope, will be to help decision-makers better understand those 401(k) plan issues that demand attention and informed decisions.

To date, the challenge of 401(k) decision-makers has been to encourage employees to participate. Now, a subtle shift is taking place, and the growing challenge is to see that the plan offered to participants is one that best meets their needs while at the same time remaining cost-effective for the plan sponsor. Designing a new plan or changing an existing plan is becoming the focus of company decision-makers as they struggle to choose from a number of options and a variety of 401(k) vendors. In many cases, we are dealing with the "layers of the onion" syndrome. What may appear on the surface to be a cost-effective and potentially popular 401(k) plan may have hidden costs or compliance problems that only a well-informed decision-maker will be able to appreciate.

When he was 15, my son, Mason Butler, an immodest, self-described "great golfer," was finally talked into taking a lesson from a real golf pro. The pro first asked, "Mason, on a scale of one to ten, how good a golfer do you hope to become (ten being a touring professional)?"

Mason said, "I want to be an eight."

Wayne, our pro, then said, "Well, that's great. If you had said 'three' or 'four,' I would have made a few changes to tune up your existing swing and your golf would have improved a little bit, but you would never have become great. Now, because you said 'eight,' I have a license to completely change your swing and start from scratch to correct all your bad habits. This lesson is going to ruin your existing game, but it's the first and necessary step to getting you where you want to be in this sport."

The purpose of this book, like Mason's golf lesson, should be to provide a basic lesson in the fundamentals of the 401(k) plan. You may not enjoy some of what you read, because you may learn that you are now saddled with the by-product of some previous bad decisions. They may be costly to change and an embarrassment to admit, but changes are generally cheaper and easier to make when the plan has $500,000 of assets than when it has grown to $2,000,000.

It's easier (and cheaper) to change Mason's golf swing at age 15 than waiting until he's a middle-aged duffer with a burning desire to put together a presentable game of golf. In the case of your 401(k) plan, yesterday's bad decision may someday lead to the plan's disqualification and taxation of all of its assets, plus penalties—and, possibly, the loss of your job if you were responsible.

This book may not be a favorite of those in the pension sector of the financial services industry. If you're like every other decision-maker, you are receiving one or two calls a week from people trying to sell you some aspect of a 401(k) plan, so keep the cloves of garlic around your neck and a copy of this book right by your phone. After all, it's always possible that the right vendors will call, and you will be able to identify them by asking the right questions.

Better yet, you may learn that you have long since installed the perfect plan with the right vendors. In either case, I hope to deliver up some tips that will improve your game.

This book is divided into two parts. Part One discusses the basic operation of 401(k) plans, including:

1. Why they are so popular

2. How they work

3. How to design them

4. How to promote them to employees

Part Two discusses how to select and pay for administrators, investment managers, financial institutions, attorneys, and certified public accountants for the plan.

A final chapter of Part Two discusses more specialized issues related to 401(k) plans, such as using 401(k) plans in partnerships as opposed to regular corporations. This last chapter offers a glimpse at the many other issues that come into play as we operate these programs. They are typically not critical to the design and operation of the average 401(k). Generally speaking, the decision-maker will be paying other professionals to sort through these ancillary issues.

In short, this book offers a readable collection of the basic concepts, as well as many useful tips, which will lead to a 401(k) plan that best meets the needs of your company, its employees, and yourself as both decision-maker and plan participant.

Stephen J. Butler
February 1995
Lafayette, California

Acknowledgments

I want to acknowledge the help of many people on this project, but a key contributor has been my business partner of almost twenty years, Theodore Kao. He has demonstrated a natural inclination toward understanding the complex matrix of tax and labor regulations that essentially create the pension administration industry. His ability to use these concepts creatively and effectively has always provided me with a "product" that I could help our clients understand and use effectively.

I also want to acknowledge John Diamante, my biology lab partner some 30 years ago at Harvard, who worked with me once again to encourage me to write this book. His organizational effort and persistence were significant factors in launching this effort and locating a publisher.

Charles Dorris, a seasoned business writer and editor, has been especially helpful in the challenge of compressing some 28 chapters of information down to an economical 15 without diminishing the content in any way.

Finally, there are my two families:

There are my associates at Pension Dynamics Corporation whose prodigious efforts keep these plans on track. Working with this group offers a daily affirmation of how much intellectual energy and industry knowledge is demanded of a plan that by all outward appearances is operating smoothly. While I think everyone at our company is great, I have a special appreciation for some key people who have been with our company for many years, such as Melania Budiman, Julie Sambo, and Ilona Shakibnia. Our technical consultant, Cheryl Morgan, was also especially helpful in the writing of this book.

My other family is the one at home. My wife, Fran, and my children Elsa and Mason, have offered much encouragement and have been supportive throughout—as well as my parents, William and Elsie Butler, whose general advice I continue to receive and enjoy.

PART ONE

BASICS

Part One of this book explores the basic operation of 401(k) plans, including

- **The reasons behind their increasing popularity**

- **How they work**

- **Various considerations in their design and implementation**

- **How to promote (sell) them to employees in different situations**

Chapter 1

Why 401(k) Plans Are Popular

A 401(k) plan is the most popular type of pension plan that any company can offer today. Graph 1-1 shows the phenomenal growth of 401(k) plans during the 1980s, when many large companies created these plans. At this writing, of the 80,000 companies with 100–1,000 employees, 31% have 401(k) plans, and of the 4,500 companies with more than 1,000 employees, 82% have 401(k) plans.

Today, it is small companies (those companies with fewer than 100 workers) that are fueling a steady growth in 401(k) plans. And there is plenty of room to grow. Studied indicate that 90% of all Americans work for companies with 100 or fewer employees. And Access Research, the Connecticut consulting firm, reports that there are 1,700,000 companies, which employ between five and 100 employees, and less than 10% of these companies have 401(k) plans today.

To understand how 401(k) plans can be used, the first step is to understand why they are so popular with employees and employers. This chapter explains that popularity.

‖‖‖ EMPLOYEES WANT 401(k) PLANS

401(k) plans are popular among employees because

1. Workers are disillusioned with conventional pension plans
2. Americans are aging and becoming more savings- and retirement-conscious
3. Most Americans are in surprisingly high marginal tax brackets on the last few dollars of income

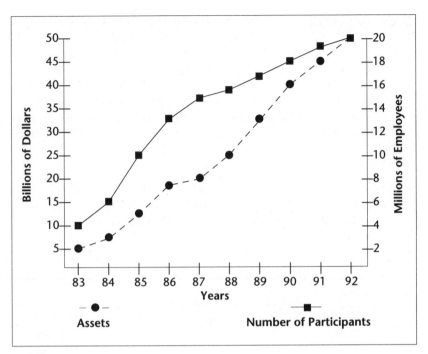

Graph 1-1

4. Many Americans desire greater financial security in these uncertain times—and in the distant future, because Social Security appears to be falling short of expectations

5. These plans inspire employee participation

Disillusionment with Conventional Pension Plans

Conventional defined-benefit and profit-sharing plans have become the dinosaurs of the pension industry. Why has this happened? Why would employees prefer a benefit they have to pay for over conventional plans funded entirely by their employers? Why would anyone look that gift horse in the mouth?

The answer: The working patterns of Americans are changing, and as a result, too many people have received the short end of the stick from company pension plans that never generated any meaningful retirement benefits.

Why have conventional pension plans failed today's workers? Most pension plan features were established by laws dating back to the days when employees spent a lifetime working for one company. Today, working patterns are entirely different. The average employee changes jobs five times during a career. Women joining the work force—and working sporadically while combining careers with motherhood—have little opportunity to stay with one company long enough to qualify for fully vested pension benefits.

Vesting schedules and other aspects of conventional pension plans do not fit today's work patterns and penalize younger workers.

Vesting Schedules   An example shows the problem created by vesting schedules. An employee has worked four years for a company with a retirement plan that has the following seven-year vesting schedule.

Vesting Schedule

Year One	0%
Year Two	0%
Year Three	20%
Year Four	40%
Year Five	60%
Year Six	80%
Year Seven	100%

At the end of year four, the employee has an account balance of $20,000—assuming that employer contributions and plan earnings have averaged $5,000 annually.

However, based on the vesting schedule, if this employee leaves the company after four years, the employee can keep only 40% or $8,000 ($20,000 × 40%).

The "nonvested forfeiture" (in this case, $12,000) reverts to the plan and is divided among the remaining employees or credited against the employer's next annual contribution. To keep the entire account balance, the employee in this example must stay at this job for three more years.

But, what about the "golden handcuffs" aspect of that vesting schedule? Won't it encourage this employee to continue working long enough to become fully vested?

Dream on! For most employees, especially younger ones, money in a pension plan is often too abstract to be a deciding factor in their decision to stay with a company. Ironically, only when employees leave the company and are paid their vested account balance do they realize that the plan was worth real money. But, by then, it is too late to influence their decision to stay or leave. The payout usually occurs at least eight months after the employee leaves, and, in some cases, only when the employee reaches retirement age, some 40 years and several jobs later!

So, in an age when high employee turnover is the norm, vesting schedules meet the needs of neither the employee nor the employer.

Penalizing Younger Employees   In addition to the small benefits produced by vesting requirements, traditional defined-benefit plans penalize younger employees. These plans are funded to meet specific benefits upon retirement. For young employees, a plan sponsor can contribute very small amounts in the early years of their employment; there is enough time until retirement for these small contributions to compound and fund the retirement benefit. When younger employees change jobs and leave these plans, they are always shocked at the small size of their "accrued benefit."

This disappointment is apparent when I talk to rank-and-file workers in small companies with traditional pension plans. Most of these plans are set up to accommodate the tax planning needs of the owners and managers. That rank-and-file employees receive little or nothing is considered incidental.

401(k) Plans and Today's Work Patterns   In the face of shifting work patterns, the 401(k) plan offers employees a tremendous opportunity: a *portable* pension plan that they know with 100% certainty can be scheduled to meet their retirement needs. By comparison, receiving a benefit from a conventional plan is more like playing the lottery. Paul Yakabosky, of the Employment Benefit Research Institute in Washington, D.C., is quoted by columnist Jane Bryant Quinn in the *San Francisco Chronicle* as saying, "A well-invested 401(k) can give you a higher retirement income than a classic pension."[1]

With so much uncertainty about the practical application of conventional pension programs, the introduction of the 401(k) concept was like a breath of fresh air. Because IRAs, which offer some of the same benefits as 401(k) plans, have been historically under-

subscribed, government officials have been surprised at how popular 401(k) plans have become.

For example, President Reagan, with his Tax Reform Act of
1986, originally tried to do away with 401(k) plans. By that time,
however, an influential voting block of more than ten million Americans participated in these plans. He was advised that trying to end
401(k) plans would be a mistake. Within the first few days of the
introduction of the tax bill's first draft, the part calling for the end
of 401(k) plans was deleted.

Since then, 401(k) plans have only increased in popularity.

An Aging Population

Demographically, the timing could not be better for 401(k) plans.
The World War Two baby boomers, now in their mid to late for-
ties, make up a "demographic bubble" moving through society.
They are suddenly realizing that retirement is only about 20 years
away. Many are in their highest earning period, spouses have gone
back to work, and children may be out of school; there is now some
discretionary or extra income for retirement savings.

According to a survey reported in the *San Francisco Chronicle*
(9 January 1994), the most popular New Year's resolution across the
United States was to save more money.[2] The imperative to save by
a major portion of our population is enormous, and this accident
of timing makes 401(k) plans the right financial vehicle at the right
time.

High Tax Brackets

With both state and federal income taxes levied against most Americans, it doesn't take much income these days to be in that 33%
tax bracket on the last few dollars of income. Any single person
with adjusted gross income of more than $17,434 and any married
person with family income of more than $34,907 will pay taxes (or
save taxes) at the 33% rate beyond those income levels—at least in
those states (such as California and New York) with healthy state
income taxes.

Most other states have at least some state income tax, but
even someone paying no state income tax can generate a substantial retirement benefit by using a tax-advantaged 401(k) plan. A person need not be a major league baseball player or a neurosurgeon
to have tax problems or to appreciate tax savings.

More Financial Security

I think we would all agree that when people are considering careers or jobs, job security is often more important than salary. But, with job security at an all-time low in private industry, people are struggling to fill this gap in their financial security with their own resources.

A 401(k) plan offers what is effectively a government subsidy (given the tax savings) for people trying to build a financial nest egg as quickly as possible.

Inspiring Employee Participation

Compared to conventional retirement plans and IRAs, 401(k) plans have characteristics that excite employees and produce high rates of employee participation.

Employer Promotion of 401(k) Plans   Employers must make 401(k) plans attractive and understandable to rank-and-file employees before management can participate. Thus, employers go to elaborate lengths to promote the plans, even in some cases offering matching contributions. Employers have no such incentive to promote IRAs.

Significant Employee Contributions   Compared to contributing $2,000 to an IRA, employees can contribute to a 401(k) plan up to 20% of their pay or a dollar maximum of $9,240 in 1994. A 401(k) plan is a serious opportunity to save for retirement.

Employee Borrowing   Employees can borrow from their 401(k) accounts, thereby turning them into a tax-advantaged savings plan, which can be used for expenditures like home down payments and college tuition. While few employees actually borrow, the borrowing opportunity removes the psychological impediment to locking money up in a long-term retirement program, especially for younger people who see retirement as a distant abstraction.

Employees As Investors   401(k) plans often acquaint employees, for the first time, with equity-oriented mutual funds. These mutual funds offer excitement and the knowledge that the employee has an investment in the stock market, an investment chosen by reasonably sophisticated trustees.

Group Dynamics   Peer pressure, the desire to be part of the group, even in a relatively small company, prompts many employees to participate. Because 401(k) plans are employer-sponsored, there is a community of "fellow savers" at work who talk about the plan each quarter when the statements come out.

Matching Contributions   The element of "winning the game" plays a role because many plans offer matching contributions, and some employees will make whatever 401(k) contribution is necessary so that no compensation is left on the table.

Ease of Automatic Payroll Deductions   We rarely miss money that we don't see in the first place. "Saving before we spend" is an automatic factor in a 401(k) plan.

IIIII EMPLOYERS LIKE 401(k) PLANS

Employers like 401(k) plans because they

1. Can be used by firms of virtually any size

2. Help recruit employees

3. Fit today's "new age" management philosophy

Suitable for Any Size Company

A company with as few as two employees can install a 401(k) plan. And, contrary to a very popular belief, 401(k) plans can be successful in small companies.

Recruiting Employees

The two most popular employee benefits today are 401(k) plans and health plans. For a group of 50 people, the health plan will cost about $150,000 per year, but the 401(k) plan will cost only about $5,000 per year. Compared to other employee benefits, the 401(k) plan is a good value. It is even cheaper than a dental plan for all but the smallest companies, and more popular with employees.

Common questions asked in many job interviews are, "What about your 401(k) plan?" "When can I join and what kind of investments does it offer?" "Can I rollover into your plan the outstanding loan from my previous employer's 401(k)?" "Can I call an 800 phone number to get my account balance?"

If 401(k) plans are second only to health plans in popularity among employees, they are obviously an important recruiting tool.

Fostering Entrepreneurial Spirit

The recent recession has forced American business to become more entrepreneurial at all levels. Companies today struggle to encourage individual initiative and decision making, because these have proven to be a more cost-effective approach to accomplishment than layers and layers of "tough management" and chains of command. And the work force has come to appreciate this fundamental truism: the only security in life stems from the ability to do something and to do it well. This applies to us as individuals as well as to the groups with whom we work.

A 401(k) plan fits perfectly, and in a fundamental way, with these new company cultures that encourage individual entrepreneurship within the corporate culture. It reinforces the need for people to take charge of their lives and accept the responsibility for their futures. The 401(k) plan presentation and promotional materials emphasize these points over and over again. These plans, then, are helping to create a new breed of responsible, self-actualized employees that all companies, large and small, are struggling to attract and retain.

As a fundamental underpinning of our society and economy, 401(k) plans could not be arriving at a more auspicious time. In the face of our national obsession for get-rich-quick schemes, 401(k) plans stand as beacons of hope. The fact that these plans have accumulated so much money in voluntary contributions and enjoy such popularity is a great testimonial to the underlying strength of the American psyche.

The decision-maker must light that 401(k) "beacon" or perhaps brighten the plan already in place. A 401(k) plan perceived by employees as a great plan becomes an important cornerstone of the corporate culture and leads, ultimately, to higher productivity through the retention of the right employees.

In a broader sense, then, the magic of 401(k) plans may extend beyond retirement plans. They could be the foundation of a new era of decentralized or "down-loaded" (as opposed to "downsized") management as we move into the twenty-first century.

||||||||||||||||||||||||||||||||||||||||||||||||||||||||||||||||||||||||||||||||||||||||
SUMMARY

401(k) plans have grown dramatically because they meet the needs of today's workers and employers, and conventional pension plans do not.

401(k) Plans Fit Today's Work Patterns

- For today's mobile work force, traditional pension plans do not provide meaningful benefits, and vesting schedules do not increase employee longevity.

- Compared to traditional pension plans, 401(k) plans are portable—a feature that fits today's work force.

401(k) Plans Fit Today's Financial Requirements

- As baby boomers age, they become more concerned about saving for retirement.

- As more Americans move into higher tax brackets, they are attracted to the tax-advantaged savings that 401(k) plans offer.

- Compared to IRAs, 401(k) plans allow much larger contributions by employees.

- 401(k) plans allow employees to borrow from their accounts for purposes other than retirement, thus turning 401(k) plans into real savings plans.

401(k) Plans Fit the Needs of Employers

- Because companies with as few as two employees can install 401(k) plans, the plans are versatile and well suited for small companies.

- As 401(k) plans become popular with employees, the plans become an important way to recruit employees.

- Compared to health care plans, 401(k) plans are inexpensive, and are the most cost-effective employee benefit that companies can offer.

- As companies strive to instill an entrepreneurial spirit into their employees, they can use 401(k) plans as an element of this "new age" approach to management.

Notes

[1] Paul Yakabosky, quoted by Jane Bryant Quinn, in "Surprising Good News on Baby Boomers Retirement," *San Francisco Chronicle*, (17 October 1994), Business Section, p. D7.

[2] Eric Tyson, "Your Money Matters," *San Francisco Sunday Examiner and Chronicle*, (9 January 1994), Business Section, page E1.

Chapter 2

How 401(k)
Plans Work

Before decision-makers present a 401(k) plan to employees, and even before they formally design it, they should understand how a plan works.

This chapter discusses the basic workings of a 401(k) plan. Chapter Three then discusses the tests that plans must pass to qualify for their tax-advantaged status. And Chapter Four discusses two aspects of 401(k) plans that companies can elect to include: allowing plan participants to borrow from their accounts and offering matching contributions.

The basic operation of a 401(k) plan has five aspects:

1. Significant contributions can be made to 401(k) plans

2. Contributions receive favorable tax treatment

3. The plans are flexible and portable

4. The plans have a relatively simple structure

5. The plans offer professionally managed investment choices

ⅢⅢ SIGNIFICANT AMOUNTS OF MONEY CAN BE CONTRIBUTED

For 1995, the maximum contribution to a 401(k) plan is 20% of a participant's income or $9,240, whichever is less.

That any one participant can contribute up to 20% of compensation into a 401(k) plan confuses many people who have always heard that the maximum is 15%. To clarify this, for any one participant the maximum contribution is 20%, but for an entire 401(k) plan, the *average* contribution cannot exceed 15%. So, if in the unlikely event all participants in a plan contribute 20%, the entire group's contributions must be reduced until the average for the group does not exceed 15%.

The 20% of compensation that can be contributed in behalf of a participant and the 15% of compensation that can be contributed in behalf of the entire 401(k) plan may consist of three segments:

1. The participant contribution

2. Any employer matching contribution

3. Any contribution into a profit-sharing plan

The following diagram illustrates these different segments of contributions and how the maximum percentages apply.

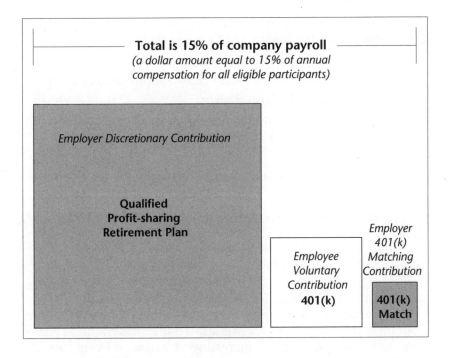

Two examples illustrate how this segmenting of contributions work: first, for the entire 401(k) plan and, second, for one participant.

Segmenting Contributions for a Group of Participants

To illustrate the segmenting of contributions for a group of employees, assume that contributions into the first two segments are as follows:

1. The average contribution of all participants   6%

2. An employer matching contribution of
    50 cents per $1 of the participants'
    average contribution   3%

    Total   9%

How much can the employer contribute to the profit-sharing plan for the entire group of employees?

    Because 15% of compensation is the maximum that can be contributed to all three "compartments" of the plan, the employer can contribute up to 6% (15% minus 9%) into the profit-sharing section of the plan.

Segmenting Contributions for One Participant

To illustrate the segmenting of contributions for one participant, assume that contributions into the first two segments are as follows:

1. The participant contribution   9.0%

2. An employer matching contribution of
   50 cents per $1 of the participant's
   contribution   4.5%

3. Employer contribution to profit-sharing   6.0%

   Total   19.5%

This participant has received contributions that are within the 20% allowed.

    But what if all participants received total contributions of 19.5%? The plan would be overfunded because the maximum for participants as a group is 15%. Contributions would have to be reduced until the average for the group was not more than 15%.

    In addition to the percentage maximums on contributions from these three segments, there is also a dollar maximum: $22,500. This maximum will not be increasing at a cost-of-living rate. As stated earlier, a participant may contribute up to $9,240 (in 1995) to the 401(k) plan (the first segment), but the participant may receive not more than $22,500 annually from all three segments.

    Decision-makers must monitor both the percentage and the

dollar contributions to the 401(k) plan and any other matching or profit-sharing contributions made to the participant.

IIIII CONTRIBUTIONS TO THE PLAN RECEIVE FAVORABLE TAX TREATMENT

Employees contribute to a 401(k) plan by voluntarily reducing their salary and depositing money equal to the amount of the reduction into the plan. No federal or state taxes are paid on the money deposited. All investment earnings on these deposits accumulate in the plan on a tax-deferred basis.

The advantages of 401(k) plans cannot be disputed. The value of the favorable tax treatment alone is enormous. Two examples can demonstrate this.

Spendable Income Versus Savings

The first example shows what a participant gives up in spendable income compared to what the participant accumulates by contributing this income into a 401(k) plan.

To calculate the amount saved in the 401(k) plan, assume

1. A participant contributes $150 per month for 20 years into a 401(k) plan.
2. The savings earn an average annual return of 8%. (This may seem high by today's standards, but during the past 60 years, the annual stock market return has averaged 10%.)
3. By the end of year 20, the savings in the plan have accumulated to $88,353.

To calculate the amount of spendable income that the participant forgoes, assume

1. The participant (in California at least) is in a 34% combined state and federal tax bracket at the margin. (This would be a single taxpayer with adjusted gross income of more than $17,454—$34,907 if married—in 1994.)
2. The $150 equals $99 after tax ($150 × 66%).
3. During the 20 years, the participant forgoes $23,760 of spendable income ($99 × 12 months × 20 years).

The employee forgoes $23,760 and accumulates $88,353.

Saving in a 401(k) Plan Versus Saving After-Tax Dollars

A second example shows how much more an employee can accumulate in savings by using a 401(k) plan compared to using after-tax dollars. In this example, assume

1. An employee saves $150 per month for 20 years in a regular savings plan.

2. The savings earn an annual rate of 8%.

3. The employee pays combined federal and state taxes at a rate of 34%.

Using after-tax dollars in a regular savings plan, the employee accumulates only $42,034. This compares to $88,353 using the 401(k) plan.

The basic arithmetic of 401(k) accumulation, as highlighted by these examples and the following chart, is so positive that it is almost unbelievable!

- Forgo $35,640 of spending money during a 30-year period and wind up with $223,553.

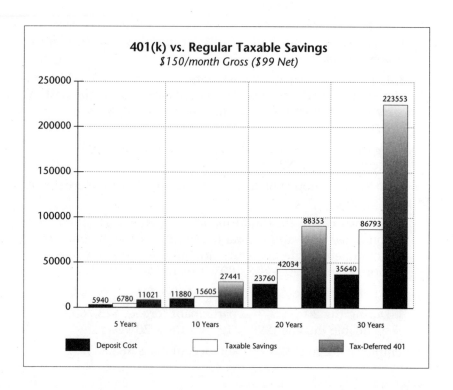

401(k) vs. Regular Taxable Savings
$150/month Gross ($99 Net)

- Save almost 3 times as much after 30 years using a 401(k) plan as using an after-tax savings plan.

Yet, 401(k) plans can accomplish this, thanks to the magic of compound interest operating in a tax-deferred environment.

IIIII 401(k) PLANS ARE FLEXIBLE AND PORTABLE

Participants in a 401(k) plan can withdraw money from their accounts for the following reasons:

1. Termination of employment
2. Hardship or financial need distribution
   a. Purchase of a home
   b. Unreimbursed medical expenses for the participant or a dependent
   c. Educational expenses for the participant or a dependent
   d. Prevention of participant eviction or mortgage foreclosure
   e. Funeral expenses for family member
3. Reaching an age of more than 59½ years
4. A loan to the participant

Upon participants' retirement or termination, they can have the funds from the 401(k) plan distributed to them in several ways:

1. Receive funds in a lump sum and pay regular taxes on the money in one of several ways:
   a. If under age 59½, the participant will pay regular taxes plus federal tax penalties of 10% and (in California) state tax penalties of 2%.
   b. If over age 59½, the participant incurs no penalties but pays taxes as follows:
      i. The funds are considered the participant's only income. They are not added to any other income of the participant for purposes of calculating taxes.
      ii. Funds can be income-averaged over five or ten years depending on the participant's age.
2. Leave the funds with the former employer's 401(k) plan.

3. Roll over the funds into an IRA or into the new employer's 401(k) plan.

In options two and three, the tax obligation is further deferred, and earnings continue to build with no annual tax obligation.

With the portability of 401(k) plans and the flexibility to continue deferring taxes, the participant can enjoy tax-advantaged savings for long periods of time and accumulate a large pool of capital.

IIIII 401(k) PLANS HAVE A RELATIVELY SIMPLE STRUCTURE

The structure of a 401(k) plan has the following building blocks:

1. A retirement plan trust fund

2. A plan document

3. A summary plan description for plan participants

4. The filing of an IRS form 5500 each year

5. The investment choices for the plan in keeping with U.S. Labor Department regulation 404(c)

6. A plan sponsor

These features will be covered in great detail in later chapters, but a short description of them at this early stage may help the decision-maker understand the "flesh and bones" of a 401(k) plan.

The Legal Structure of the Plan

A Retirement Plan Trust Fund   This is the legal entity (much like a corporation) that houses the assets of a 401(k) plan and separates them from the money in the company that sponsors the plan. A retirement plan trust fund is controlled by trustees of the plan, who are usually the same people who own and run the company (in smaller companies anyway).

A Plan Document   This document dictates how the plan will be operated: who is eligible, matching contributions, and loans, etc. The document is extremely important. An improperly signed document, for example, is a cause for plan disqualification.

A Summary Plan Description   This is the official description of the plan (as opposed to the promotional material) that, by law, must be provided to all participants. It describes, in lay terms, what the plan's general provisions are. It also points out that participants have the right to review all plan documents by writing to the Labor Department in Washington, D.C.

IRS Form 5500   This is the annual report to the government that lets it keep tabs on the plan. The plan's balance sheet and income statement are reported on this form as well as the number of participants and other information regarding the plan's activity during the year. An IRS audit of the plan always centers on a review of the form 5500 for a specific year.

Investment Choices   Investment choices for the plan receive a great deal of attention. Generally, these investments are mutual funds, which are selected by the trustees after obtaining advice from a variety of sources.

Trustees can limit their liability by offering at least three different types of investments and demonstrating that they are providing participants with adequate information about the investments.

Plan Sponsor   The plan sponsor is the corporation or business entity that offers the plan to its employees. The plan sponsor ultimately controls all aspects and decisions of the plan not dictated by the government. The responsibilities of the plan sponsor are performed by the trustees of the plan.

IIIII PLANS OFFER PROFESSIONALLY MANAGED INVESTMENT CHOICES

Most participants wind up with better investment performance in their 401(k) plans than they would experience otherwise; there are several reasons for this.

First, the amount of money in the 401(k) plan is often substantial, enough so that the best investment advisors can be hired, advisors who are more skilled than the smaller-scale financial planners who work with individual employees.

Second, most successful business owners and senior managers, who are the trustees selecting the investments, are reasonably sophisticated. Many know what to expect from the investment advisor's recommendations and are less likely to be seduced by overnight riches that might be promised to individual employees.

Third, business owners and senior managers know that a great deal is at stake: their own money is invested in the plan, and they don't want to look bad in the eyes of their employees.

The bottom line: the employee gets access to well-researched investment advice, provided with no sales commission if no-load mutual funds are the investment choices.

The selection of investments and investment advisors will be discussed in detail in Part Two of this book.

|||||||||||||||||||||||||||||||||||||||||||||||||||||||||||||||||||||||||||||||||||
SUMMARY

Before designing a 401(k) plan or promoting it to employees, decision-makers must understand several basic characteristics.

401(k) Plans Allow Substantial Contributions

- Participants can contribute the lesser of
  - 20% of their annual compensation, or
  - $9,240 (in 1994), which is adjusted annually based on a cost-of-living increase.

401(k) Plans Receive Favorable Tax Treatment

- Contributions to the plan reduce taxable income, and contributions earn income on a tax-deferred basis.
- Favorable tax treatment allows participants to accumulate savings much faster than in a regular savings account.

401(k) Plans Are Portable

- When participants leave a company, they can
  - Be paid the account balance in a lump sum and pay taxes on the distribution

- Leave their 401(k) account balance with the former employer and continue to enjoy a tax-deferred treatment

- Roll the account balance into an IRA or the new employer's 401(k) plan and also continue to enjoy a tax-deferred treatment.

401(k) Plans Have a Legal Structure

- A retirement trust fund is established to house the plan's assets, separate from the company sponsoring the plan.

- The plan document specifies how the plan is to operate.

- The plan sponsor is the company sponsoring the plan; and it is represented by a group of trustees who are usually company owners, board members, or senior managers. The plan sponsor is the plan's principal decision-maker.

401(k) Plan Investments Are Professionally Selected

- The amount of money in the plan is often enough to attract the best investment advisors.

- Company owners, senior managers, and investment advisors select investments for the plan.

Chapter 3

401(k) Plan Testing

The general rationale for all pension legislation is to force or encourage company owners and top managers to offer pension plans to their employees if the owners and managers want to enjoy the benefits of these plans.

To assure that lower-paid employees are not discriminated against, the 401(k) plan must pass certain discrimination tests. If the plan fails these tests, it may be disqualified, with all participants losing their tax-advantaged benefits, and the company or its owner may be assessed heavy penalties.

This chapter discusses three common discrimination tests:

1. Average Deferral Percentage (ADP) Test

2. Top-Heavy Test

3. Coverage Tests

▖▖▖▖▖ THE ADP TEST IS THE BASIC DISCRIMINATION TEST

The basic discrimination test in a 401(k) plan is the Average Deferral Percentage (ADP) Test. It guarantees that the contributions of the lower-paid employees are related to those of the highly compensated employees. Before the ADP Test can be completed, the highly compensated employees in the company must be identified.

Identifying the Highly Compensated Employees

Participants in the 401(k) plan who the IRS calls "highly compensated employees" or HCEs consist of several groups:

1. The owners of 5% or more of the company and any corporate officers making more than $60,000 in 1995.

2. Any employees making more than $100,000 in 1995.

3 Employees who are in the top 20% of the payroll and make more than $66,000 in 1995. To identify this group, simply list employees in the order of annual salaries and draw a line delineating the top 20%. For example, if there are 100 employees eligible for the plan, the line is drawn at 20 employees from the top. Any of the 20 employees who make more than $66,000 is an HCE.

4. Employees who are family members (a spouse, child, or parent) of HCEs, regardless of their compensation.

5. Employees who were HCEs during the prior year, regardless of their income during the current year.

The dollar amounts above are applicable during 1995 and in most cases are adjusted each year based on a cost-of-living increase.

Having identified the HCEs, everyone else in the company is a "non–highly compensated employee" or NHCE.

Running the ADP Test

In running the ADP Test, first determine the percentage of compensation that NHCEs as a group contribute to the 401(k) plan, i.e., their average percentage contribution.

The following example illustrates how the average is calculated in a company with eight NHCEs:

Non–Highly Compensated Employees

Participant	Salary	Dollar Contribution	Percentage Contribution
A	$10,000	$500	5%
B	15,000	0	0%
C	20,000	2,000	10%
D	30,000	1,500	5%
E	30,000	2,400	8%
F	40,000	800	2%
G	40,000	2,000	5%
H	45,000	2,250	5%

Total 40%

NHCEs' Average Contribution 5%
(40% divided by eight employees)

After determining that the average contribution for NHCEs in this example is 5%, the next step is to determine the average contribution percentage allowed the HCEs.

There are three formulas for doing this. The formula used in a specific case depends upon the NHCEs' average percentage contribution:

1. Greater than 2% and less than 8%

2. Less than 2%

3. Greater than 8%

Greater Than 2% and Less Than 8% If the average contribution of NHCEs is greater than 2% and less than 8%, the HCEs can contribute an average of two percentage points more than the NHCEs' percentage contribution.

This formula applies to the example above, because the average NHCEs' contribution is 5%. The HCEs can contribute an average of two percentage points more than the NHCEs or 7% of compensation (5% + 2%).

In the example, further assume that the company has two HCEs who are company owners. Do their average contributions meet the test?

Highly Compensated Employees

Participant	Salary	Dollar Contribution	Percentage Contribution
A	$70,000	$7,000	10%
B	$80,000	$3,200	4%
			Total 14%
		HCEs' Average Contribution 7%	

The test is passed because the average HCEs' contribution of 7% is within two percentage points of the average NHCEs' contribution of 5%.

The HCEs in this example could do a little "horse trading" and swap percentage contributions to some extent. If Participant A agreed to drop to an 8% contribution, then Participant B could move to 6%; their average contribution would still be 7%. All the test demands is that their average not exceed 7%.

The formula illustrated above is the most commonly used. However, the two other formulas apply when the average percentage contribution for the NHCEs is less than 2% or greater than 8%.

Less Than 2%   If the average NHCEs' contribution is less than 2%, the average HCEs' contribution is limited to double the NHCEs' average percentage contribution.

For example, if the NHCEs contribute an average of 1.5%, the HCEs can contribute an average of not more than 3%.

More Than 8%   If the NHCEs' average percentage contribution is greater than 8%, the HCEs' average percentage contribution is limited to 1.25 times the NHCEs' average.

For example, if the NHCEs' average contribution is 9%, then the HCEs can contribute an average of not more than 11.25% (9% × 1.25).

To summarize the average percentage contributions:

Average Percentage Contributions

Average NHCEs' Contribution	*Average HCEs' Contribution*
Less than 2%	Not more than two times NHCEs' contribution percentage
2% to 8%	Not more than two percentage points more than the NHCEs' contribution percentage
More than 8%	Not more than 1.25 times the NHCEs' contribution percentage

If a plan fails an ADP Test, a portion of the contributions must be returned to highly compensated participants. How this is accomplished will be discussed in a later chapter.

Also to be discussed later is the term "Multiple Use Test," which crops up in two situations: when a matching contribution is less than 100% vested and when there are voluntary after-tax 401(k) contributions. The latter are legal but virtually nonexistent because of their lack of popularity.

||||| THE TOP-HEAVY TEST ALSO LIMITS KEY EMPLOYEES

In a 401(k) plan, key employees cannot have in their accounts more than 60% of the entire assets of the plan. If their accounts exceed 60%, the plan is "top heavy," and if not corrected, the plan is disqualified, and participants lose all tax benefits.

Key Employees

Key employees are not to be confused with highly compensated employees, even though the definitions are similar. Key employees consist of four groups:

1. Any officer whose annual compensation exceeds $60,000 (in 1995)

2. Each of the ten employees who own the largest percentage of the business, but excluding those who do not own more than 0.5% of the business and whose annual compensation does not exceed $30,000

3. All employees who own more than 5% of the business, regardless of annual compensation

4. All employees who own more than 1% of the business and whose annual compensation exceeds $150,000

Where Top-Heavy Problems Occur

Top-heavy plans can occur in smaller companies or in companies with many owners such as law firms. They can also occur in companies that once had pension plans in which key employees built up substantial account balances; because, even if the former plan was terminated four years ago and the money was rolled into IRAs for the key employees, those roll over account balances are still included in the Top-Heavy Test, thanks to a five-year "lookback" provision in the law.

Solving a Top-Heavy Problem

To solve a top-heavy problem, the company can make a "top-heavy minimum" contribution for all "non-key" employees of at least 3% of their annual compensation. A second solution is to exclude the key employees from participation until their account balances become less than 60% of the entire plan's assets.

The Top-Heavy Test is important, but it often gets overshadowed by the ADP Test. However, the top-heavy issue is becoming increasingly critical as more smaller companies offer 401(k) plans.

IIIII COVERAGE TESTING CONTROLS ELIGIBILITY CHOICES

Companies may exclude or carve out from their 401(k) plans some groups of employees, such as seasonal workers, who would probably not contribute to the plan anyway. Employees not contributing to the plan bring down the average percentage contribution of non–highly compensated employees and, thus, they reduce the contribution opportunity for highly compensated employees.

However, for a plan to be qualified, a certain proportion of a company's employees must be eligible. To make sure that this requirement has been met, Coverage Tests must be passed. Coverage Tests and carving out will be discussed in Chapter 5.

IIIII THERE ARE GOOD REASONS FOR TESTING

The 401(k) plan is a marvelous financial instrument, offering many employees one of their best opportunities to create financial security. However, to prevent disqualification of the plan and/or heavy penalties against the company sponsoring the plan, it is critical to obey the law religiously.

One look at the complex Labor Department and IRS regulations should convince decision-makers that the government is earnest in encouraging companies to make these plans attractive to employees. The discrimination tests required of 401(k) plans are accomplishing this purpose. They are one of the most elegant and successful attempts at social engineering ever devised by the federal government; there is now no movement to substantively change them.

Correctly performed testing is the cornerstone of a successful plan. To an extent, testing may be a nuisance and a nemesis, but decision-makers should appreciate that the need to pass the tests is what has made these plans so successful. Has anyone ever seen the savings plan of a company-sponsored credit union promoted as aggressively as a 401(k) plan? Surely not. It doesn't happen because it doesn't need to happen.

Decision-makers must also understand the basics of testing

because it is the engine that drives so many 401(k) plans. The greater the participation by rank-and-file employees, the greater the benefit to company owners and senior managers.

As will be discussed in succeeding chapters, this need for rank-and-file participation is the rationale for allowing loans for any purpose, offering popular investment choices, promoting the plan aggressively, and allowing employees to participate after working for only a short time.

‖‖‖

SUMMARY

For the 401(k) plan to be qualified and provide tax benefits, the plan must not discriminate against lower-paid workers in favor of higher-paid workers. To enforce this rule, the government requires that the plan pass discrimination tests. Failing these tests results in the plan's disqualification, the loss of tax benefits, and possible penalties against the company sponsoring the plan.

The ADP Test Is the Basic Discrimination Test

- The ADP Test assures that the contributions from highly compensated employees are based on the contributions from non–highly compensated employees.

- To correct a failed ADP Test, a portion of the contributions are returned to the participants.

The Top-Heavy Test Controls Key Employees

- When the assets of key employees make up more than 60% of a 401(k) plan's assets, the plan is top heavy, and special limitations or regulations are triggered.

- A top-heavy problem can be corrected by the company contributing to the accounts of all non-key employees an amount equal to 3% of compensation.

The Coverage Tests Regulate the Eligibility of the Plan

- A company can exclude or carve out groups of employees from being eligible for the plan.
- A minimum percentage of the company's employees must be eligible for the plan to pass the Coverage Tests.

Chapter 4

Loans and Matching Contributions

Chapter 2 discussed the basic characteristics of a 401(k) plan. This chapter discusses two additional aspects that companies can elect to include:

1. The ability of participants to borrow from their accounts
2. The offering of matching contributions by the company sponsoring the plan

IIIII EMPLOYEES CAN BORROW

While the 401(k) plan ostensibly helps participants save for retirement, it also allows participants to borrow money from their accounts for goals short of retirement.

The average 401(k) participant has more than 20 years before retirement. However, eyes would glaze over in a room full of typical employees if only a retirement plan was discussed. Many in the workplace need to save for their children's college educations and down payments for homes. Some may need to save just to have a financial cushion, if they work in a cyclical industry. For these people, the loan provision removes a psychological impediment to depositing money into what would otherwise be strictly a retirement plan. This barrier is why relatively few people use IRAs to the maximum degree.

The loan provision works well because participants can focus on achieving a financial goal short of retirement itself. They use the plan to reach that interim goal, pay the loan back, and then go on to the next major financial accomplishment. Finally, they are ready for retirement, after having deposited into their account substantial sums of interest that would otherwise have been paid to banks in a series of loans. (The average $15,000 automobile purchase triggers bank interest payments of about $10,000 over the five-year life of the loan. As discussed below, employees pay interest on loans from 401(k) plans right back to themselves.)

By offering an avenue to achieve interim goals, the 401(k) plan can compete with the many consumer products and services that younger people are tempted to buy. Participants gain tremendous satisfaction from knowing that they are saving responsibly.

The Purpose of Loans

There is much confusion regarding the purposes for which loans are permitted, because many plans do not allow loans or limit the purposes for which they can be made; some plans allow loans only for down payments on primary residences.

To minimize the "hassle factor" of loans, these plans remove one of the greatest attributes of the 401(k) plan, especially from the perspective of younger employees.

The law, however, is very clear: participants can borrow from their 401(k) plans *for any reason.*

The Amount of Loans

Participants can borrow 50% of their account balance, up to a maximum loan of $50,000. There is no minimum loan amount.

Participants can borrow more than 50% in some cases. If their account balance is under $10,000, for example, participants can borrow their entire account balance. However, to the extent that their loan exceeds 50% of their account balance, they need to collateralize any excess amount (the amount over 50%) with a house, car, or savings account. For example, a participant with an $8,000 account balance can borrow all $8,000, but $4,000 of the loan must be collateralized. Or, if a participant with a $10,000 account balance borrows $6,000, the first $5,000 (50% of $10,000) requires no collateral, but the remaining $1,000 of the $6,000 loan requires collateral. The maximum loan, in any situation where the loan balance is going to be more than 50% of the account balance, is $10,000.

At first glance, this expanded loan limit may not seem worth the effort, but it can significantly improve the overall contribution level of lower-paid employees. Here is the reason why: many younger employees want to use the plan to save for a down payment on a home. If they mistakenly thought that they could only borrow half of their account balance, they might forget the 401(k) plan, pay their taxes, and save what was left—a much more tedious and less cost-effective way to save. Knowing they can borrow their entire account balance prompts them to use the plan, which increases participation and the chance that the plan will pass its tests.

Interest Rates and Loan Terms

The interest rate paid on the loan is determined at the outset and must be comparable to the rate charged by a local financial institution for the same type of loan. Generally, the rate is about two percentage points higher than the prime rate. Ultimately, the plan trustees determine the interest rate on a loan, using comparable current rates as a guideline.

The term of the loan can be a maximum of five years, and it must be fully amortized with payments at least quarterly. (In other words, no balloon payments at the end of five years are allowed.) If the loan is used to purchase the participant's primary residence, a term of up to 20 years is permitted, and early repayment on all loans is always an option.

How Loans Are Made

When a participant borrows from his or her 401(k) account, some of the account's assets are liquidated, and the proceeds loaned to the participant. The loan becomes an asset of the participant's account, in effect, another investment that the participant has chosen.

The interest paid on the loan is credited to the participant's account. The interest is not deductible by the participant for tax purposes, but it is treated like any other income of the plan and enjoys the same tax-deferred compounding.

Loan Repayment

Loans are typically repaid through an automatic deduction from the participant's salary, so that if the participant is working, the loan is automatically kept current.

If a loan goes into default while the participant is working for the company, very serious plan qualification problems result. Technically, a loan in default is an unauthorized withdrawal from the plan, so avoiding defaults is imperative. Insisting that all loans be repaid by automatic payroll deduction is the best insurance policy. As long as a participant is working, the loan is guaranteed to be kept current. If he or she terminates employment, they can borrow conventionally to pay back the loan, or they can take the unpaid loan balance as a portion of their 401(k) distribution. Because the loan balance cannot be rolled into an IRA, it will be treated as income to the employee and will trigger a tax obligation.

Loan Fees

Never pay anything toward the cost of a participant loan. The administrative cost of setting up a loan ranges from $75 to $100 and is generally paid by the borrowing participant—not the employer. The plan sponsor, then, should pass on any administrative cost of loans to the participant. This would mean a fee of about $75–100 to set up the loan and $50 per year to administer it. If collateral is involved, add $200.

These fees create a better barrier to excessive use of loans than limiting loans by dollar amounts or any other means.

The Infrequent Use of Loans

In practice, participants do not borrow money from their accounts as often as one would expect. In my experience as a pension administrator, I have seen only about 5%–10% of participants actually borrow from their accounts at any given time. Surprisingly, this percentage has not changed that much over the years. I would have expected it to increase as participants accumulated more money.

I don't have an answer for this, but my best guess is that 401(k) money becomes sacrosanct in many participants' minds. They would rather borrow conventionally than tamper with their 401(k) money. Also, there can be an opportunity cost: if the participant borrows from an investment returning 12% annually and the participant pays only 8% on the loan, he or she misses out on a net 4% of return on the outstanding amount of the loan.

A Flexible Loan Policy Versus Hardship Distributions

As was mentioned in Chapter 2, there are only two avenues for a participant who is still working to remove money from a 401(k) plan: borrowing or a hardship distribution.

Hardship Distributions   While loans can be for any reason, hardship or financial need distributions are limited to three "safe harbor" purposes:

1. Purchase of a primary residence
2. Educational expenses for the participant or a dependent
3. Unreimbursed medical expenses for the participant or a dependent
4. Funeral expenses
5. Avoiding eviction or mortgage foreclosure

Apart from the safe harbor provisions, plan sponsors may elect to broaden their plan's definition of a hardship. However, this can be risky, because if the IRS later determines that a distribution was not a hardship, it may disqualify the plan. In practice, approving hardship distributions beyond the safe harbor can become a rubber stamp exercise, because the average plan sponsor does not want to stand between participants and their 401(k) money.

This difficult issue was discussed in 1989 at a Western Pension Conference in San Francisco, where I sat on a panel with human resource professionals and lawyers from a collection of major Silicon Valley Fortune 4,000 companies. They were talking about how difficult it was to "play God" as they struggled to determine what really qualified as a hardship distribution. Some of them elected to hear each participant's story and determine if it qualified for a hardship distribution. Was a new engine for the car that the participant used to get to work an acceptable hardship?

I suggested that the best antidote to the hardship definition problem was to simply liberalize the loan provision.

The Cost of Hardship Distributions   Borrowing from a 401(k) plan is a wonderful way to avoid paying taxes and penalties on a hardship distribution. Many participants hear the word "hardship" and naturally assume that there are no penalties or taxes associated with the distribution. *Not so!* Participants taking a hardship distribution will pay taxes at their highest marginal tax rate, because this distribution will be over and above what they already earn. For most participants, the combined federal and state income tax rate will be about 34% at the margin. Then, there will be a federal penalty of 10% and typically a state penalty of about 2%. The combined cost of a hardship distribution approaches 50% for most participants.

There is an additional cost. A participant who takes a hardship distribution must wait a year before making any further contributions to the plan. And once the money for the hardship distribution has been removed from the plan, it cannot be returned; future contributions are limited to the standard annual contribution.

Therefore, in addition to the taxes and penalties, the participant also incurs the opportunity cost of having removed money from the plan that could otherwise have been compounding on a tax-deferred basis.

Loan Policy Versus Hardship Distribution   The harder we look at hardship distributions, the more attractive the loan provision looks by comparison. A plan sponsor who fails to offer a liberal loan provision is only driving the participants into the expensive realm of the hardship distribution. And, as participants lose interest in the plan, the plan begins to fail the discrimination tests. All too often, the plan sponsor's knee-jerk reaction to this is to increase the matching contribution rather than to liberalize the loan provision. Increasing or adding a matching contribution might cost $10,000 to $20,000 a year. Liberalizing the loan provision might cost $150 for a plan amendment. The smart plan sponsors' rule of thumb: never tamper with the matching contribution until you've liberalized loans to the maximum.

The loan provision is a wonderful way to remove the taxes and penalties incurred if money has to be withdrawn from the account to make a crucial expenditure; with the loan, the participant goes on achieving his or her savings goals.

And if participants pay the entire cost of the loan, why should anyone care whether they borrow or why they borrow? Let the free market handle the situation. What plan sponsor wants to play God, unless he or she just doesn't have enough to do?

IIIII EMPLOYERS CAN OFFER MATCHING CONTRIBUTIONS

Some of the most costly 401(k) design decisions center on matching contributions. And the benefit of matching contributions on the plan is too difficult to measure accurately.

Matching contributions are not needed for a successful 401(k) plan. However, in some instances, matching contributions can improve 401(k) plan performance. To determine when to use matching contributions, the plan sponsor must understand the right and wrong reasons to offer matching contributions, and the right and wrong types of matching contributions to offer.

The term "Matching Contribution" applies to any contribution that the employer makes that results from a voluntary employee contribution. It can be a dollar-for-dollar match or, for example, a match of ten cents for each dollar of contributions.

The Wrong Reasons for Offering Matching Contributions

Matching contributions are often mistakenly used as a form of incentive compensation and as an incentive to participate in the 401(k) plan.

Matching Contributions As Incentive Compensation   Under the basic philosophy of compensation, employees are paid because they work hard. They are paid a bonus when they work extra hard, when they develop additional skills and/or experience, or when a division or the entire company has a year of great performance. Ideally, these factors should be the only basis for any bonus or raise.

Companies with a 401(k) matching provision are effectively giving a bonus based solely on an employee's ability to contribute to a 401(k) plan, which may create an inequity. For example, two employees equally deserve a bonus, but only the one contributing to the 401(k) plan receives the matching contribution; the other employee, who may have just bought a house and has no discretionary income to contribute, loses out.

On one level then, a 401(k) matching contribution flies in the face of basic compensation strategy and common business sense.

Matching Contributions As an Incentive to Participate   The basic argument for a matching contribution is that it increases participation in the 401(k) plan and improves the possibility of passing the ADP Test.

However, many 401(k) plans with no matching provision pass their ADP Tests, and the outcome of the tests appears unaffected by the matching contribution. Advertisers say that "50 percent of what is spent on advertising is wasted, but you never know which 50 percent." A match is a significant 401(k) cost component, and much of it probably goes to employees who would have contributed anyway.

The Wrong Type of Matching Contribution

When matching contributions are offered, they are often accompanied with a vesting schedule, so that the matching contribution is not immediately 100% vested.

Vesting Schedules as a Way to Reduce the Cost of the Plan   Just like the vesting schedule in a traditional pension plan (discussed in Chapter 1), vesting schedules with a matching contribution require the participant to stay with the company for some number of years before having the right to all of the matching contribution. If the participant leaves the company before becoming 100% vested, the non-vested portion is forfeited and credited toward future company matching expenses. On paper, this should reduce the cost of the match over time.

However, the company does not benefit from the non-vested forfeitures for at least a few years, until participants are actually forfeiting material amounts of money. In the meantime, the matching contribution is costing the full amount of the commitment.

And, the forfeitures will never amount to much in a company with relatively low turnover among employees with one year or more of service.

Matching contributions are expensive, and vesting schedules do not reduce their cost significantly.

Vesting Schedules as a Creator of Problems   In fact, vesting schedules create two problems. First, a matching provision with a vesting schedule is difficult to communicate to employees. In the middle of an otherwise great employee presentation about saving taxes and saving money, it must be stated, "We interrupt this great program to point out that you forfeit money if you don't stay with the company for a certain length of time."

Having to insert this element of negativity detracts from the momentum of the promotional effort. Vesting is difficult to describe in just a few short minutes. Some employees come away with the mistaken impression that if they don't stay with the company long enough, they forfeit some of *their own* 401(k) contributions.

Second, if a matching contribution is not immediately 100% vested, the plan must pass the 401(m) Test. This additional test compares the percentage of matching contributions that are vested for the non–highly compensated employees with those that are vested for the highly compensated employees. This creates a potential problem: in a typical company, HCEs are further along on the vesting schedule than the average NHCEs (where there is more turnover). This explains why plans often fail the 401(m) Test, even if they pass the basic 401(k) (ADP) Test. And if they fail the 401(m) Test, HCEs receive money back as taxable income.

This additional "Multiple Use Test" increases administrative costs, not to mention the hassle of amended personal tax returns in some cases.

The Right Reason for Offering Matching Contributions

If a company wants to offer a retirement benefit to only those employees who, by their voluntary 401(k) contributions, have demonstrated that saving for retirement is important to them, a matching contribution can meet this need.

All too often, companies spend money on conventional retirement plans that employees—especially younger ones—couldn't care less about. And, any money spent on compensation that employees don't recognize as being of value is just money wasted. At least a 401(k) matching contribution is guaranteed to be recognized and appreciated, because it is only received by employees contributing their own money to the plan.

A matching contribution is probably the most cost-effective form of company contribution to a qualified retirement plan. The only retirement plan more cost-effective is a 401(k) plan with no company matching contribution.

The Right Kind of Matching Contribution

If a company wants to offer a matching contribution, probably the best formula involves a relatively small contribution that is capped at an annual dollar amount and is immediately 100% vested. This encourages as many employees as possible to use the 401(k) plan to some extent.

Using this formula, a company might contribute 25 cents for every dollar contributed by the participant; the matching contribution would be capped at an annual amount of $100. Thus, a participant depositing at least $400 would receive a matching contribution of $100.

This formula was used in a concert production company in which most stagehands and production employees made an average of $6 per hour; 87% of the employees eligible for the plan contributed at least $400 per year, because they couldn't stand the thought of leaving the $100 matching contribution on the table.

So, if a matching contribution is considered, it should be

1. Immediately 100% vested

2. Relatively small

3. Capped at an annual dollar amount per employee

These three rules keep the plan simple with costs under control.

Otherwise, the confusion and controversy surrounding matching contributions often creates a tragedy: the matching contribution becomes the "deal point" that stalls the momentum toward offering a 401(k) plan. If decision-makers believe that a 401(k) plan without a match is a waste of time, they will rob themselves and their employees of tax deductions and tax-deferred compounding.

A "minimalist" approach to the matching contribution, such as the $100 example above, may generate higher contributions and a more popular plan at a very reasonable increased cost.

Decision-makers must remember that once matching contributions are in place, they are difficult to change. Like any employee benefit, they become an entitlement in the eyes of the employees, and removal can hurt morale. A bad decision about matching contributions can cling to the plan like a barnacle, and generate an ongoing expense that dwarfs all other costs of the 401(k) plan.

SUMMARY

Allowing participants to borrow from their 401(k) plans is one of the most important and yet most underrated factors in a successful plan. On the other hand, an employer matching contribution is one of the most expensive and overrated factors in a plan.

The Ability to Borrow Is Crucial to a 401(k) Plan's Success

- Loans can be made for any purpose.

- Loan amounts are 50% of the account balance up to a maximum loan of $50,000; however, participants can borrow 100% of the first $10,000 in their accounts.

- Loan interest rates are comparable to those of local financial institutions, and the loan term can be up to five years, and up to 20 years for the purchase of a primary residence.
- Without a liberal loan policy, participants who need to withdraw money from their accounts are forced to use hardship distributions, which carry draconian taxes and penalties.
- In practice, few participants borrow from their accounts, but the ability to borrow is a crucial element in the plan, especially for younger participants who are saving for financial goals short of retirement.

Matching Contributions Are Not Needed

- Matching contributions are costly and may not increase employee participation in the plan.
- Vesting schedules with matching contributions do not decrease the cost of the matching contributions. Further, they are difficult to explain to employees, and they can create the need for the 401(m) Test.
- If a matching contribution is offered, it should be immediately 100% vested, be relatively small, and be capped at an annual dollar amount per employee.

Chapter 5

Designing a 401(k) Plan

Keep a 401(k) plan simple to start with, and then promote the need to save money and save taxes. These are the two keys to successful 401(k) design and promotion.

This chapter discusses the basic rules for designing a simple 401(k) plan and the pitfalls to avoid in the design process.

To keep the plan simple,

1. Restrict eligibility as much as possible

2. Do not include matching contributions

3. Allow loans for any purpose

4. Operate the plan on a calendar year whenever possible

5. Promote the plan every year

6. Use popular mutual funds for the investment choices

7. Do not underestimate employee sophistication and desire to save

8. Promote and design the plan simultaneously

IIIII RESTRICT ELIGIBILITY

The key to designing a plan that will pass 401(k) discrimination tests is the eligibility requirement: how long the employee must work for the company to be eligible for the 401(k) plan, and which employees will be eligible to participate.

The reason for restricting eligibility is as follows: if the plan is available to only employees likely to participate, the plan usually has a better chance of passing the discrimination tests; for example, employees with several years of service are more likely to participate in a 401(k) plan than are newer employees.

Remember, all employees who are eligible for the 401(k) plan but who contribute nothing are considered part of the plan for testing purposes. Enough of these employees can drag down the average percentage contribution for non–highly compensated employees and limit the contributions of highly compensated employees.

Choosing correct eligibility requirements, then, lays a solid foundation for a smooth-running plan that passes tests and meets expectations. Also, more restrictive eligibility reduces the administrative costs of processing short-term employees.

What clouds the thinking of plan sponsors is that they want their plans to accommodate newly recruited employees. They want to say that the 401(k) plan is available, especially to new key management people. Here is how you solve that problem and also maintain the one-year eligibility period.

First, maintain the one-year eligibility period for contributions but allow new employees to roll over previous 401(k) account balances into your plan immediately. This allows them to use the borrowing feature of the 401(k) plan without interfering with the testing requirements.

Second, remind new employees that they have the legal right to leave their money in their prior employer's 401(k) account (if they have more than $3,500). Many employees are bullied into believing that they must take their money, which is simply not true.

Third, if they are not eligible to contribute to your plan for one year, they can contribute to an IRA and receive a full deduction; the inability to contribute is not as large an opportunity cost as it might otherwise seem, if new employees are reminded of this.

Fourth, when employees do become eligible for your plan, even if only in the fourth quarter of the year, they can contribute up to 20 percent of their entire year's compensation. For example, an employee making $50,000 per year and becoming eligible during the fourth quarter of the year could contribute $1,666 out of each $2,083 paycheck during the last six pay periods of the year.

Fifth, employees are often too anxious to roll over money that would be better off in a rollover IRA. An employee's own IRA with a collection of pure no-load mutual funds will often effect infinite investment flexibility compared to a 401(k) plan that has a limited choice of investments and administrative costs that are passed on to the employee. Ideally, an employee should roll over old account balances into a new employer's 401(k) plan *only* when one of two needs arise:

1. The employee wants to access the funds through the 401(k) plan loan provision, which is not available with an IRA

2. The employee wants to take advantage of five-year income averaging on a lump sum distribution after age 59½, which is also not available in an IRA

Employees need to appreciate that once the money is rolled into the new 401(k) plan, it cannot be rolled back into an IRA until they terminate employment. This one-way street presents limitations that many employees don't appreciate until it is too late.

The Eligibility Period

To participate in a 401(k) plan (to be eligible) typically requires one year of service. The employee joins the plan at the beginning of the calendar quarter following the twelfth month of service. For example, an employee who started working on August 1, 1994, would complete the twelfth month of service on July 31, 1995, and be eligible to join the plan on October 1, 1995.

If the company wants to cover only full-time employees, the twelve-month period must include at least one thousand hours of service for the employee to qualify as full-time.

It sometimes makes sense to choose a short eligibility period during the initial enrollment period of a 401(k) plan. During this time, everyone is talking about the plan, and there is a great deal of positive momentum. Later, as new employees become eligible one-by-one, that same enthusiasm is difficult to impart, and the sign-up ratios can begin to drop. When this happens, simply change to a one-year waiting period for employees hired after the initial enrollment period.

For any eligibility period shorter than one year, there is one serious complication: the one thousand hours of service requirement can no longer be used. A plan with, for example, a 90-day eligibility period must include everyone who works even one hour per week, if they have worked 90 days. If a company has seasonal employees who come back each year during the harvest or during the Christmas season, these employees are eligible for the plan after the first year. However, they will not be inclined to participate and will drag down the testing results. Thus, eligibility periods of less than one year can be useful, but must be used carefully.

Having championed the cause of the one-year eligibility period, I must acknowledge that some companies do just fine with shorter eligibility periods. A company that passes its ADP Tests with wide margins can afford to pick whatever eligibility period it wishes. A company that is not overly concerned with the plan's administrative costs can also be more cavalier about allowing shorter-term employees to be eligible.

In my experience, however, many plan problems and expenses are minimized in the long run by choosing the longest possible eligibility period. Remember, most people selling 401(k) plans have an interest in building up the number of participants. The "assumed close" in the marketing exercise is often a 90-day eligibility period. That revolving door of employees who come and go within a year may increase overall costs by as much as 20 percent. Look at your own company's turnover and arrive at your own estimate.

Eligible Employees

In addition to the period of service, eligibility can be restricted as to the employees covered. To exclude employees unlikely to participate, companies are allowed to carve out up to 30% of their work force. A company may want to exclude permanent part-time employees who work more than one thousand hours per year or employees in a remote division halfway across the country. If these people are excluded, they are not considered part of the plan for testing purposes.

Understanding carve-out techniques is important, because decision-makers are often amazed, if not blindsided, by whom they are required to include in the plan. The seasonal workers mentioned previously are one issue, but even independent contractors, in some situations, can be considered part of a group controlled by the company and thus eligible for the plan.

The decision-maker must begin to design the plan with a clear understanding of who is eligible, and then carve out groups of employees to confine the plan to those who are most likely to contribute.

The Rules of Carving Out   Section 410(b) of the Tax Code allows a retirement plan to be qualified as long as at least 70% of the non–highly compensated employees are eligible for the plan:

> The percentage of non–highly compensated employees covered under the plan must be at least 70% of the percentage of highly compensated employees covered under the plan.

For example, if 100% of a company's highly compensated employees are covered—which is typical—then 70% of the non–highly compensated employees must be covered.

Employees can be carved out as long as the plan document spells out clearly which groups of employees or which company division is being excluded. Specifically named employees cannot be carved out. Instead, for example, all clerical employees and groundskeepers can be excluded.

Carving Out Highly Compensated Employees   In most cases, a carve-out involves only non–highly compensated employees. However, Section 410(b) assumes that some employees who are carved out will be highly compensated. And, in fact, this may be in the plan's interest. For example, assume:

1. A company has ten highly compensated employees

2. The company wants to exclude two of them because they work across the country in a remote company outpost

3. Thus, only 80% of the company's highly compensated employees are eligible

If 80% of the highly compensated employees are eligible, the law requires that 56% (70% times 80%) of the non–highly compensated employees also be eligible. In this example, almost half the company can be carved out, thus making it more exclusive and more likely that the plan will pass the tests. Also, the plan's administrative fees have been lowered.

In some cases, it would make economic sense to carve out a few highly compensated employees and just give them a bonus made possible by the savings generated by a more exclusive plan. Or, in some companies in which the owners are so financially well off that their 401(k) contribution is not important to them, carving them out can open the door to a more exclusive plan.

There are limits to the number of employees who can be carved out: Section 401(a)(26) basically says that to be qualified a plan needs to cover the lesser of 40% of the work force or 50 employees. Plan sponsors who adopt too "minimalist" an approach and wind up with an exclusive group of overly-eager contributors may find that they have carved themselves into a plan that doesn't meet the 40% coverage requirement.

Carving Out Lines of Business To make the plan more exclusive, decision-makers can use the "separate line of business" regulations. If a division or part of a company is deemed to be in a separate business from the main part of the company that is offering the 401(k) plan, the division can have its own plan or no plan at all; that is, it can be carved out.

To be deemed a separate line of business requires meeting the following criteria:

1. At least 50 employees must be eligible for the retirement plan

2. The division to be excluded must be at least 50 miles from the main portion of the company

3. The division to be excluded must be in a decidedly different business from that of the main part of the company

These regulations were published in final form in August 1992, and because of their recent vintage, this carve-out feature has not yet been used to any great extent.

Union Employees

Union employees are almost always excluded from 401(k) plans because they usually have their own union pension plan. Major league athletes, for instance, don't participate in the team's pension plan because they have their own union plan. All employees whose contracts are the product of collective bargaining fit into this category, even if they don't belong to a union.

IIIII AVOID MATCHING CONTRIBUTIONS

As discussed in Chapter 4, a 401(k) plan does not need a matching contribution from the employer. It is best to start a 401(k) plan with no matching provision.

With no matching contribution, the plan is very simple to design and to promote. Also, removing the matching contribution removes what would have been a major cost and, ultimately, a major reason for why most "would-be" 401(k) plans have wound up "dead in the water."

ⅡⅡⅡ INCLUDE A LIBERAL LENDING POLICY

The key to a successful 401(k) plan is a liberal loan policy—a policy allowing participants to borrow for any reason and for any amount, but requiring the participants to pay loan costs. This type of policy is inexpensive, and increases participation, which is important from a testing standpoint. It removes a major psychological impediment to making contributions.

Yet, many companies have failing plans because there is no loan provision or a highly restrictive one. This leaves plan sponsors wondering why their employees won't save. In desperation, they increase the matching contribution and introduce another round of unnecessary expense for the plan.

ⅡⅡⅡ OPERATE ON A CALENDAR YEAR

Choosing a calendar year for the 401(k) plan makes sense for several reasons. First, participants think and budget based on calendar years.

Second, if a 401(k) plan's year ends, for instance, on June 30, the plan straddles two calendar years, which can make solving any problems more costly—problems such as returning excess contributions to highly compensated employees because their plan failed an ADP test. The following examples show how much easier it is to correct such a problem when the plan uses a calendar year.

Assumption: During 1995, an executive contributes the maximum dollar amount of $9,240 to the 401(k) plan.

Example A

401(k) Plan Year: January 1–December 31

1. In January 1995 after the end of the 401(k) plan's year, it fails an ADP Test and returns as taxable income $240 of the executive's contributions plus investment income.

2. The plan must return money on a first-in-first-out basis, so the $240 is assumed to have been the first money contributed to the plan, in January 1994.

3. On April 15, 1995, the executive files his or her tax return reflecting the added taxable income. There is minimal inconvenience, and the tax return is filed at the normal time.

Example B

401(k) Plan Year: July 1–June 30

1. On April 15, 1995, the executive files a tax return for the 1994 tax year reflecting the contributions to the 401(k) plan made during 1994.
2. After the plan's 1994 year ends on June 30, 1995, the plan fails an ADP Test and must return, as in Example A, $240 plus investment income to the executive.
3. The money being returned to the executive must be considered the first contributed to the plan, in July 1994, the beginning of the 401(k) plan's 1994 year.
4. The executive filed his or her 1994 tax return three months earlier and now must refile the tax return.

In the second example, the executive is probably annoyed and blames the plan's administrator for not doing a more accurate or at least a more conservative projection of how much could be contributed.

But, projections can never be totally accurate; the only test that can be accurate and the only test that counts is conducted at the end of the plan's year, when every dime of contributions from every eligible employee has been determined. In a small company, testing can be dramatically affected when a few major participants leave the company or become eligible in midyear.

However, some 401(k) plans must operate on the company's non-calendar fiscal year because the 401(k) plan has been added to an existing profit-sharing plan. Historically, a retirement plan's year usually coincided with the company's fiscal year; contributions could be calculated more easily. Any advantage this might provide today is far outweighed by the difficulties created—such as those illustrated in the above examples. Therefore, a calendar year for a 401(k) plan is strongly recommended.

‖‖‖ PROMOTE THE PLAN EVERY YEAR

Employees need to be reminded periodically of the plan's accomplishments. 401(k) plans compete with all the other ways that people are tempted to spend money. As new employees become eligible, they should receive not just a package of written 401(k) materials and an enrollment form, but also a sales talk.

The plan's best salespeople can often be the company's in-house contact person and the employees' supervisors. Some companies pay bonuses to supervisors based on how many of their subordinates contribute to the 401(k) plan. This one-time or periodic bonus, involving just a few hundred dollars per manager, is often more effective and much cheaper than a matching contribution.

When promoting a plan, then, be creative. Some firms use posters in the cafeteria, a mention in the monthly newsletter, a chart on the wall showing how the investments are doing, etc. Anything goes.

Some sage once said, "Good ideas are a dime a dozen, but it's only the ones that get *sold* that are worth anything." You can't put a 401(k) plan on automatic pilot and expect it to promote itself.

IIIII USE POPULAR MUTUAL FUNDS AS INVESTMENTS

As will be more fully discussed in later chapters, mutual funds are the investment of choice for a well-run 401(k) plan. Some plans have experimented with so-called "wrap accounts" that use individual money managers and invest in individual securities. But compared to mutual funds, wrap accounts have several disadvantages. First, they cost about 3% per year, which is subtracted from earnings. (Chapter 10 discusses the need to keep internal costs low.)

Second, wrap accounts, or any pool of money other than mutual funds, cannot be followed in the newspaper by participants and are not ranked by any of the standard mutual fund ranking services. This takes away some of the excitement of investing and, thus, of participating in the plan.

Finally, the accounting and auditing of mutual funds is easier (and ultimately cheaper) because the funds do all the work.

Mutual funds represent the investment of choice for 401(k) plans with less than $10 million in assets. If decision-makers don't use them, frustration and/or unnecessary expense will likely result.

IIIII DO NOT UNDERESTIMATE EMPLOYEES' READINESS TO SAVE

Many company owners and senior managers believe that rank-and-file employees live from paycheck to paycheck and can never save any money. Just such a sentiment was expressed by the president of a San Francisco bank who said, "We have a lot of single mothers as tellers. We make it a point to hire them because they are such motivated workers, but they only make between $15,000 and $20,000 per year. I can't imagine that they will be able to afford very much in the way of contributions."

For my own edification, I sat down with the bank's personnel officer after the enrollment process. The single mothers, who we identified as a group, were contributing an average of 13% of their pay!

By the same token, Hispanic workers have a tremendous reputation for contributing large amounts to 401(k) plans. Mexico has one of the highest per capita savings rates of any industrialized nation. That instinct to save translates into high 401(k) participation rates from Hispanic workers here in the United States. Yet, in many companies whose work force consists of a large proportion of foreign nationals, plan sponsors operate on the misconception that non-English-speaking employees will not participate in a 401(k) plan.

One way to avoid these misconceptions is to discuss with employees the possibility of offering a 401(k) plan before the plan design is complete, i.e., to promote and design the plan simultaneously.

IIIII **PROMOTE AND DESIGN SIMULTANEOUSLY**

Promoting the plan and designing the plan are part of the same exercise, and should be done simultaneously.

All too often, a 401(k) consultant will use census information on a group of employees to generate what is supposedly an ideal plan design for that group. Usually this predesigned plan includes a matching provision and some estimates of its cost based on estimated employee contributions. But no one has a clue about the likely participation and contribution rates in the specific company.

Asking the Employees

In a smaller company (under 50–75 employees), decision-makers can adopt a "wait-and-see" approach about eligibility and other design components and make a final decision after seeing how many and which employees wish to participate.

The presentation of the plan can be prefaced by pointing out that no final decision has been made about offering the plan. However, if enough employees express an interest, the company will then pay to have the plan installed and administered.

There is probably a psychological advantage gained by suggesting that a benefit will *not* be offered unless there is enough participation. As human beings, we all are inclined to be more interested in something that is not automatically handed to us. Also, some peer pressure will be brought to bear if some employees really want the plan and realize that they have to talk it up with their fellow workers before it can happen.

In some cases, decision-makers may find that a handful of relatively new employees would like to make substantial contributions. These may be employees who would not have qualified under a one-year waiting period. As discussed earlier, beginning the plan with an eligibility period of less than one year (to include these high contributors) may generate a better test in the first year. Thereafter, a one-year eligibility period could be installed for all new employees.

The Mistake of Sending a Memo

Caution: don't let the decision to install a plan hinge on a memo passed out to employees. Some employers say that they have taken "a survey" and that nobody is interested in a 401(k) plan. The survey is often nothing more than the question, "Do you want the company to take some money out of your pay for a savings plan?" Products and services are not sold this way, and neither is a 401(k) plan.

Make sure that employees are "voting" based on a substantive and full presentation of the plan. Chapter 6 discusses what a complete presentation of the plan needs to include.

In some cases, a plan is designed best when the design and promotion are combined, turning the employee promotional meeting into a "fact finding" session. Explain the plan to employees in its simplest form and use the enrollment exercise to gauge the level of interest. The process of designing and promoting moves ahead in a tandem fashion, which leads to an optimal plan from the standpoint of participation and company cost.

IIIII AVOID DESIGN PITFALLS

All too often, the installation of 401(k) plans is unnecessarily delayed, or even derailed, in the design stage by a mistaken focusing on three issues:

1. Choosing investments

2. Calculating the cost of a matching provision under varying scenarios

3. Trying to minimize participant borrowing

The cause of this mistaken focus: choosing the wrong type of organization to help design the plan.

Investment People Are Not Always the Best Designers

A financial institution that sells investments is not always the best designer of a 401(k) plan. The institution wants as much money as possible contributed to the plan, so it naturally tries to sell the employer on a matching contribution, even though a plan might have been very successful without one. The substantial cost of a matching contribution may prompt employers to delay the plan or not offer it at all.

As a pension administrator, I have been amazed at how many companies of 25–75 employees have no pension or 401(k) plan. In most cases, the reason given is, "We couldn't afford a matching contribution, and everyone said it wouldn't work without a matching provision." In these situations, I have always been able to install a 401(k) plan without a matching provision. In cases where the testing fell a little short, my clients (the company owners) could only contribute $5,000 a year instead of $8,000–$9,000. Is the glass half empty or half full?

In addition to wanting as much money as possible contributed to the plan, financial institutions want as little money as possible to be taken out of the plan. I often see financial institutions suggesting that loans be limited to a far greater extent than the law requires. The reason, of course, is that loans reduce money under management and are competition for the investments that the financial institution tries to sell. This is a double-edged sword because investment institutions do not appreciate that a liberal loan provision clears the way for larger contributions to the plan and, ultimately, more money for investments.

Traditional Pension Administrators Also Are Not Ideal Designers

Traditional pension administration companies often have trouble with 401(k) plans.

Many administration companies have been slow to recognize the differences between 401(k) plans and conventional pension plans. For example, in a conventional pension plan, all investment decisions are made by the trustees, and participants receive annual statements well after the end of the year—statements that tell them their contributions, vested amount, and total account balance. If a participant leaves a company and has a vested account balance to be paid out, the pension administrator can conduct the payout in a leisurely fashion, taking as long as 18 months from the date of termination.

By comparison, an administrator of a 401(k) plan typically generates quarterly reports to participants. These participants see, and occasionally change, their investment mix. They can borrow from their accounts, and if they leave the company, they will want their money *immediately*—not a year or so after their termination date.

Some pension administration firms have gravitated more easily toward 401(k) plans. The decision-maker should choose a firm based upon its 401(k) reputation. The number of plans the firm has designed and its use of a standard plan are probably the best indications that the firm knows what it is doing.

The standard plan indicates that the firm has learned the hard way that you can't please everyone and do it cost effectively. The firm has experimented and arrived at a workable formula. Beware the administrator who offers to do whatever you want.

Even Decision-Makers Are Not Ideal Designers

Some decision-makers believe that a specific 401(k) design component must be incorporated into the plan so it will have their personal stamp. It is like the auto industry senior executive who changes the design of a new car model a little bit just to feel involved.

A classic example of this syndrome can be the issue of eligibility. If decision-makers are new with their companies and want plans in which they can participate right away, they will choose a short eligibility period, something less than a year of employment. This suddenly triggers the need to include in the plan some part-time employees who are unlikely to contribute and who will drag down the results of the testing.

Human resource people often lean toward 401(k) plans that offer the most professional looking (read: expensive) materials for employees, because they feel that this reflects more favorably on their department. This is understandable, but a four-color folder with elaborate inserts has nothing to do with investment results.

Even if the decision-maker's design component is one that may lead to problems, the pension administrator, who is only trying to be accommodating, will shrug off what he or she knows may be a ticket to disaster and hope that everything will work out.

To help design the plan, select people with demonstrated experience and be aware of the biases of the designers, including those of the decision-maker.

SUMMARY

If decision-makers appreciate the complexity of the design process, they will understand that the greatest on-going cost of a 401(k) plan could be the opportunity cost of a missing design component that would have made the plan more cost efficient. These plans are not cookie-cutter commodities. Every company's demographics, and therefore its needs, are different, and these differences should be reflected in the design of the 401(k) plan.

Here is a good rule of thumb about plan design: in the beginning, keep the plan as simple as possible and as exclusive as possible. After a year or so, improve it (as to coverage testing) by allowing more employees to be eligible. Or add a small matching contribution; then, and only then, should this additional element and its cost to the plan be considered.

Adhering to these design tips will improve the probability of a trouble-free plan with high satisfaction among rank and file employees and some powerful tax benefits for owners and senior managers.

To paraphrase from the film *Field of Dreams,*

If you build it, they will come.

To get employees to come to a 401(k) plan, the decision-maker should keep the plan simple by following these rules:

Restrict Eligibility as Much as Possible

- Use a one-year eligibility period, except perhaps during the initial enrollment period.

- Carve out employees who are unlikely to participate in the plan.

Do Not Include Matching Contributions

- 401(k) plans do not need matching provisions to be successful.
- Matching provisions add considerable cost to the plan and calculating this cost can delay implementing the plan.

Allow Loans for Any Purpose and in Any Amount

- The law allows loans for any purpose.
- A restrictive loan policy undercuts the plan's popularity, especially with younger employees.

Operate the Plan on a Calendar Year

- The 401(k) plan does not need to operate on the same year as the company.
- Using a non-calendar year causes major complications if contributions ever need to be returned to participants.

Promote the Plan Every Year

- New employees must be sold on the plan.
- Assign responsibility of the sales effort to specific employees, such as supervisors.

Use Popular Mutual Funds for Investment Choices

- Mutual funds perform their own accounting and auditing functions, thus reducing the cost of using them.
- Participants can keep up with their investments on a daily basis through newspapers and mutual fund rating services, thus increasing the excitement of investing.

Do Not Underestimate Employees' Desire to Save

- Avoid misconceptions about employee attitudes.
- Employees today want to save, if not for retirement, for major purchases or college tuition.

Promote and Design the Plan Simultaneously

- Hold a meeting with employees to discuss the possibility of offering the plan and gauge employee interest.
- Modify the design of the plan based on feedback from employees.

Avoid Design Pitfalls

- Choose a plan designer based on the firm's reputation and experience with 401(k) plans.
- Be aware that financial institutions and traditional pension administration companies have biases that affect their recommendations about design, such as investment choices, matching contributions, and loan provisions.

Chapter 6

Promoting a 401(k) Plan

Chapter 5 discussed the advantages of promoting and designing the 401(k) plan simultaneously. Promoting the plan starts with an employee meeting, which creates a favorable first impression of the plan, positive momentum toward its acceptance, and employee excitement and discussion about the plan.

This chapter discusses the keys to a successful meeting:

1. Hold the meeting during working hours and make attendance mandatory

2. Choose the right person to make the presentation

3. Remember that the meeting is a sales presentation

‖‖‖ CAREFULLY SELECT TIME AND PLACE

The employee meeting is a sales presentation, and the decision-maker must select the right "stage" and create the right atmosphere.

The meeting should be conducted during working hours, and attendance should be mandatory. Thus, all employees hear the presentation, and because it is held during working hours, they are impressed about the importance of the plan to management.

It is often better to conduct several employee meetings; the groups are then smaller, which creates better question-and-answer opportunities.

The format of the meeting should include a slide or overhead presentation, which is described later in this chapter; a question-and-answer session; and distribution of written materials explaining how the plan works, its investment choices, etc.

IIIII CAREFULLY SELECT THE PRESENTATION PERSON

Carefully select the individual making the presentation. This person plays a significant role in the success of the plan.

Employees, like all humans, base their decisions on emotional feelings about a situation, and then they pick whatever rationale supports what they feel like doing.

Many employees are anxious about having money taken out of their pay to begin with. The last thing they need is to be confronted with a personality who leaves them with a vague (or not so vague) feeling of distrust. Consequently, the person who presents the plan must be reasonably charismatic and come across as believable, knowledgeable, and honest.

The person making the presentation is almost always from the firm selected to administer the plan. The decision-maker should try to meet the person to see if he or she passes the "smell test" for honesty. Who needs a version of "Joe Isuzu" destroying the final presentation of a plan that, up to that point, represents a lot of the decision-maker's time and effort?

Even though the presentation will be made by the administration firm, the decision-maker should maintain control of the presentation's content and format. The remainder of this chapter discusses these aspects.

IIIII MAKE THE MEETING A SALES PRESENTATION

A primary purpose of the meeting is to promote the plan, and to do this effectively, the decision-maker must create an agenda that reflects the three fundamental steps in marketing:

1. Create the need.
   Point out why people will have a difficult retirement if they don't start saving now.

2. Show how the product meets the need.
   Describe how every aspect or advantage of the 401(k) plan meets the employees' needs better than any other savings vehicle.

3. Close the sale.
   Discuss why the participant should sign up and begin participating today, even if they contribute very little in the beginning.

The following description of the slide presentation and the other parts of the employee meeting will elaborate on these marketing fundamentals. Too many 401(k) presentations focus only on the mechanics of the plan. They fail to create the need, and they fail to motivate employees to start participating now. In short, they put everyone to sleep.

The Slide Presentation

The slide show portion of the employee meeting should be about 20 minutes long. It should explain the mechanics of the 401(k) plan and get people excited about saving money and saving taxes. This is not the time to get bogged down in discussing different investment choices.

The slide or overhead presentation should follow these steps:

1. Discuss why people should save money, why saving is so difficult for most people, and why the 401(k) plan works where most other financial formats fail.

2. Demonstrate how the 401(k) plan operates, such as how money is deducted from employees' pay before taxes are calculated, the amount of the contribution, and how contribution amounts and investments can be changed quarterly. (The earlier chapters in this book can provide much of this information.)

3. Show some examples of compound interest, such as those in Chapter 2 (e.g., $150 saved monthly accumulates to almost $90,000 in 20 years).

    Because younger employees may be more interested in a savings program than a retirement plan, it's important here also to point out how the 401(k) plan can produce short-term results. For instance, $200 saved monthly accumulates to about $10,000 in just three and a half years.

4. Discuss the options available when employees leave the company. They should know that the proceeds from the plan can be rolled into an IRA without paying taxes or penalties.

5. Point out that money contributed into a 401(k) plan is in a retirement trust—totally separate from the affairs of the company or its owners.

    If the company goes bankrupt, the 401(k) money is

separate and safe. This is a very important point to make because many employees are apprehensive about having money deducted from their pay, and they should be assured that the money's safety in no way hinges on the solvency of the employer.

6. Discuss the conditions required for hardship distributions and loans.

Point out how impractical a hardship distribution is compared to a loan. A loan offers access to 401(k) plan money without triggering any tax or penalty, and a good 401(k) plan allows participants to borrow 100% of the first $10,000 in their accounts for any reason.

This is a critical part of the presentation because it drives home the point that 401(k) money is not locked up until retirement—that it can be accessed under very favorable circumstances. As discussed in Chapter 4, a liberal loan policy removes a psychological barrier to depositing money into a retirement plan.

7. Discuss the five- or ten-year forward averaging on lump-sum distributions. This allows the recipient of a large distribution in one year to average it with the income from four other years, thereby reducing taxes.

Point out that 401(k) plans truly shelter income from taxes and do not just defer income (like IRAs). This answers the argument that it is pointless to save taxes today if you just have to pay them eventually.

8. Illustrate the cost of waiting.

Show how much someone loses by waiting ten years to get started: for example, if a person saves $25 per week for 25 years and the savings earn an interest rate of 10% annually, the savings accumulate to about $144,000; if $25 per week is saved for 35 years and earns 10% annually, it accumulates to $403,281. The cost of waiting ten years approaches $260,000.

9. Encourage employees to begin saving today—even if they can only afford $10 per paycheck.

Emphasize that there is no minimum contribution amount. People who start with any amount usually increase their contribution at the first opportunity. People who don't start initially often never contribute.

Encourage employees to focus on a relatively short-term savings or financial goal, something that can compete with other demands for their earnings. These financial goals can be achieved by using the plan's loan provision. As the 401(k) habit is formed, the longer-term goals will take care of themselves.

Discussing Marginal Tax Brackets

The next step of the employee meeting should be a ten-minute description of marginal tax brackets. Employees should be shown how 401(k) contributions reduce taxable income.

I like to open this discussion by pointing out that "when you tell most people what they paid in taxes last year, many will say, 'I didn't pay any taxes—I got $400 back in April!' Those are the same people who say, 'How can my bank account be overdrawn when I still have some checks left?'"

As this story indicates, many employees do not understand that the last few dollars of their income are taxed at a substantially higher rate than the rate paid on their total income. Nor do they understand how high is the rate applied to the last few dollars of income when both state (if applicable) and federal taxes are considered. Without this explanation, employees who know they pay about 15% of total income in taxes will have a tough time understanding how 401(k) contributions save 36% in taxes.

Appendix C, *Marginal Tax Rates and the 401(k) Money Machine*, is my time-tested explanation of marginal tax rates. When accompanied with stories to illustrate the basic idea, this worksheet provides many employees with their first true understanding of how tax rates work.

To illustrate important points during the slide presentation and the discussion of marginal tax brackets, use stories. For example, most people are dissatisfied with their ability to save and manage money; with 10% more income, they say their problems would be solved. Contributing to a 401(k) plan can get employees that extra 10%.

Here's another good illustration to use when describing the loan provision: the average person buying four cars during 20 years will probably spend more than $30,000 on car loan interest. Employees who save enough in their 401(k) plans to become their own bankers will keep that interest as part of their financial cushion or retirement nest egg.

It's important to aim the presentation at employees least likely to contribute—younger, lower-wage employees—because their contribution percentages become the engine that drives a successful plan, a plan that passes its ADP Test with all highly compensated employees contributing as much as they wish.

Discussing Investment Choices

Because the presentation should emphasize the basic mechanics of the 401(k) plan, it is often a mistake for the meeting to center on investment choices and the characteristics of different investments.

Also, at least half of all 401(k) contributions (and, probably two-thirds to three-quarters of contributions by the younger, lower-wage employees) goes into investments that guarantee principal. Therefore, why talk about the investment philosophies of different mutual fund managers? The participants interested in that portion of the discussion are already sold on using the plan. Why waste precious airtime singing to the choir?

The few minutes spent talking about investment choices should review the guaranteed investment and the past performance of the mutual funds selections. Decision-makers are paddling upstream if they choose funds with high loads and lousy ratings in *Forbes, MONEY, Morningstar,* or *Mutual Fund Forecaster*. As discussed in Chapter 5, decision-makers should pick funds that everyone has heard of and whose past performance will help sell the plan.

Another topic to touch on is investment mix. The best advice: employees should first decide when they will need the money contributed to the plan. If saving for a home downpayment in the near future, they should lean toward the guaranteed investment. If saving for a longer-term (beyond five years) goal, they will be better served (at least statistically) by growth-oriented or balanced mutual funds. (Point out that over time stocks have returned an average of 6% per year more than money market investments.)

Tell employees, "Remember, choosing between different mixtures of cash and stock investments is an exercise in deciding whether you want to eat well or sleep well. If you don't need the money for a long time, you can choose only stocks and still eat *and* sleep well."

Appendix B provides a more thorough discussion about basic investment advice, and it can be copied and handed to employees.

To anticipate and maybe diffuse the anxiety that early 401(k) participants might experience if their mutual funds drop in value, a short discussion of dollar-cost averaging is important.

It's a good time to say, "If you're just beginning your 401(k) experience and you've chosen the stock market mutual funds for a portion of your money, you want to pray that the market crashes. As goofy as this may sound, you'll see that your contribution each pay period will buy more and more shares of the mutual fund as the market plummets. Eventually and inevitably, the market will rise in value again, and you will have automatically bought shares at low prices that you can sell at high profits to pay for your retirement or your children's education."

Next, discuss investment choices while reviewing the enrollment form.

Discussing the Enrollment Form

The enrollment form is generally self-explanatory, and discussing it is the last part of the meeting.

This is a good opportunity to point out that the enrollment form is being used to gauge employee interest in the plan. There is no absolute guarantee that the plan will be offered unless there is sufficient interest to justify the cost to the employer. (If the employer will be paying the entire cost of the plan and if there are no commissions on the investments, these points should also be made.)

If some employees ask why there is no matching contribution, answer that these plans aren't cheap to begin with and a matching contribution winds up being a bonus for the wrong reasons: it rewards people who can afford to participate in the 401(k) plan; whereas, ideally, company bonuses should be based on job performance.

Within a week of the employee meeting, the enrollment forms should be returned and tabulated. Then, the decision-maker can conduct a projected Coverage Test to determine the degree of success the plan has achieved.

SUMMARY

In 401(k) plans, good promotion is a key to good design; if a plan is well promoted, it can succeed with just a simple design. If the plan is poorly promoted, then the decision-maker is pressured to redesign the plan to generate better results. And as the plan becomes more complicated, higher administrative costs and an unhappy decision-maker are the result.

The Employee Meeting Is a Sales Presentation

- Create the financial need to save.
- Show how the 401(k) plan meets the need.
- Show the reason to start saving immediately.

Carefully Select the Meeting Time and Place

- Hold the meeting during working hours.
- Make attendance mandatory.

Carefully Select the Person to Make the Presentation

- The person making the presentation is crucial to its success.
- Pick someone who conveys honesty and trust.

Focus the Meeting at the Employees Least Likely to Contribute

- Discuss the investment choices only briefly.
- Emphasize how the plan works.

Use the Meeting to Find Out What Employees Want

- State that the plan's implementation depends on employee response.
- Adjust the plan's design based on information learned during the meeting and from the enrollment forms.

Chapter 7

Daily Valuation Versus Quarterly Valuation

The greatest single buzzword to ever hit the pension business is "daily valuation." Nothing else comes close, except perhaps the term "401(k)" itself.

This chapter discusses daily valuation and its advantages and disadvantages compared to quarterly valuation, which is the traditional method for valuing 401(k) plan assets.

||||| QUARTERLY VALUATION IS THE TRADITIONAL APPROACH

Regardless of whether 401(k) plan assets are valued quarterly or daily, the employees' contributions are deposited into the investments selected for the plan (the mutual funds, for example). The mutual fund maintains one account for money deposited by participants in a specific company's 401(k) plan.

The difference between quarterly and daily valuation occurs at the administrator level. In a 401(k) plan that is valued quarterly, the administrator monitors only a single account for all of the plan's employees in a specific investment. The money in each investment is accounted for in this pool until the end of the quarter. Then, the plan's investments are balanced, and the gains or losses are calculated. (The balancing verifies that the deductions from each participant's pay equals the deposits into each investment, and the aggregate deductions from all participants equal the total placed in each investment.)

In the next step, the gains or losses from each pooled investment are allocated to individual participants' 401(k) accounts, which are on the administrator's database. This allocation is based on the participants' relative share of each investment. (This simple arithmetic could be done on a spreadsheet program, but pension software also time-weights the gain or loss so that participants who deposit money toward the end of the quarter do not benefit or lose from gains or losses made earlier in the quarter.)

Each participant's share of a pooled 401(k) investment is based on their cost basis in the investment at the end of the quarter; this consists of the cost basis at the beginning of the quarter plus six contributions for the six pay periods during the quarter. For example, assume that on January 1, the plan's investment in a mutual fund is valued at $94,000. During the next quarter, the plan's participants add $1,000 each pay period for a total of $6,000. On March 31, the plan's cost basis in the mutual fund is $100,000. During that quarter, the mutual fund's investments appreciate, and on March 31, the mutual fund's statement shows that the plan's account is valued at $102,500. The difference between the $102,500 value and the $100,000 cost basis constitutes a $2,500 gain. This gain can result not only from appreciation in the mutual fund's investments but also interest and dividends received from those investments.

The administrator will divide the $2,500 gain among the participants based upon their proportionate share of the cost basis in the mutual fund. To illustrate this, further assume that the account statement of Executive A shows a balance on January 1 of $9,400, 10% of the plan's $94,000 investment in that mutual fund. During the quarter, Executive A contributes a total of $600. On March 31, Executive A's cost basis is $10,000, still 10% of the total 401(k) investment of $100,000 in that mutual fund. Executive A receives 10% of the $2,500 gain and on March 31, has an account balance of $10,250.

The preceding steps, then, explain how quarterly valuation of a 401(k) plan works.

Quarterly valuation is also referred to as "balance forward" accounting, because the valuation includes the last contribution of each pay period, even though the contribution has not been deposited in the mutual fund as of the last day of the quarter. By comparison, a daily-valued plan only includes money that has been deposited and invested.

IIIII DAILY VALUATION IS THE HOT NEWCOMER

In a 401(k) plan that is valued daily, the employees' contributions are deposited into the investment and maintained as one account for the total plan—the same approach as used in plans that are valued quarterly. However, the administrator, instead of also maintaining a single account for all of the plan's employees until the end of the quarter, maintains an account for each participant and re-values that account daily, based on the change in the investment's value.

For example, assume that a pension administration firm has 500 clients (five hundred 401(k) plans) and 25,000 participants. These participants, in turn, have chosen a combined total of 50 different mutual funds. (Any one 401(k) plan will have offered five mutual fund selections, but because most plans offer different funds, these 500 client companies have chosen 50 funds.)

Every morning, the previous day's value per share of each mutual fund is entered into the employee database maintained by the administrator. Each participant's accounts will be re-valued up or down, depending upon the daily change in price of the mutual fund. All accounts are essentially balanced every day so that the employee can be informed of his or her account balance on a daily basis. Hence the term, "daily valuation."

To generate statements at the end of the quarter, the pension administration software sorts through all 25,000 participants and groups them based on which of the 500 clients they work for. Each company's participant statements are generated and mailed. Because all of the accounting for each participant has been done on an ongoing basis throughout the month, there is no additional time required for the cost-basis calculation and gain or loss calculation done in a quarterly valuation well after the end of the quarter.

IIIII DAILY VALUATION IS POPULAR AND MORE ACCURATE

The advantages of daily valuation include:

1. Popularity with employees
2. More accurate and faster allocation of investment gains or losses

Greater Popularity with Employees

Compared to traditional quarterly valuation, daily valuation is definitely more popular with employees—for two reasons. First, it allows participants to know their account value and loan limit every day, to change their investment mix on any day, and to call an 800 phone number the day after payday to find out if their contributions have been deposited.

Second, when an employee terminates participation in the plan, daily valuation allows a faster payout of the participant's account balance. If participants leave the plan during the middle of the quarter, they can be paid their account balance immediately because the account is balanced and has had investment gains or losses allocated to it daily. With plans valued quarterly, the payout occurs at the end of the quarter during which the participant left.

More Accurate Allocation of Gains and Losses

Daily valuation more accurately allocates gains or losses from investments. To understand this advantage, the decision-maker must understand the shortcomings of quarterly valuations in this regard. Misallocations can occur in two instances: when the value of investments change rapidly during a quarter; or when a participant withdraws a substantial amount of money from the plan (borrows or terminates participation) or changes the investment mix.

Rapid Changes in Value   As discussed earlier, in a plan that is valued quarterly, investment gains or losses are allocated on a time-weighted basis (the length of time the participant's money has been invested during the quarter). However, this allocation assumes that these gains or losses occurred evenly throughout the quarter. In fact, a mutual fund can gain or lose 5% in a few days. If a plan is valued quarterly, these "hiccups" in performance are not accurately reflected, and the gains or losses are misallocated.

Pension laws recognize that misallocations can happen, but the laws assume that the misallocations are a zero-sum game: any participant who loses a few cents of earnings today will get them back tomorrow when the next misallocation works in his or her favor. Daily valuation removes this characteristic of "earnings slosh" within a quarter.

Substantial Withdrawals of Money or Changes in Investment Mix
Misallocations of gains or losses can also occur when a substantial
amount of a participant's investment is withdrawn or when the
investment mix is changed.

To illustrate this, assume that a 401(k) plan includes an
investment choice (an aggressive growth mutual fund) in which
only the company president and Employee A have placed money.
As of March 31, the president's account in this mutual fund is valued at $40,000 and Employee A's account at $10,000, for a total of
$50,000.

In mid-May, the president decides to borrow $40,000 from
his 401(k) account, and his investment in this mutual fund is sold,
and the proceeds used for the loan. However, since the last quarterly valuation on March 31, the mutual fund has dropped in value
by 10%; the 401(k) plan's investment in it has declined from
$50,000 to $45,000. The president receives $40,000 from the invest-
ment because that was the value of his investment as of the last
quarterly valuation. But this withdrawal leaves only $5,000 in the
account for Employee A.

If at the end of the next quarter, on June 30, there has been
no further change in the share price of the mutual fund, the value
of Employee A's account will be $5,000; Employee A has experi-
enced a 50% loss (from $10,000 to $5,000) even though the investment itself lost only 10%.

This is an extreme example, and, in practice, one participant
rarely controls a disproportionate share of any one investment.
Also, it is not a problem in money market or guaranteed investments because these investments never decrease in value.

Finally, this phenomenon adversely affects the remaining
participants in an investment only when that investment's value is
falling, and over long periods of time, stocks and bonds have
increased in value; if an investment appreciates or produces earnings, the appreciation and earnings attributable to the money withdrawn remain in the plan, to be divided among the remaining participants in the investment.

But to some degree, this phenomenon is happening continually, as money, in any amount, is withdrawn from 401(k) plans
with pooled funds and quarterly valuations. And even if there is
appreciation and earnings, misallocations occur; in this case, the
participant withdrawing money is hurt by the misallocation. The
misallocations caused by quarterly valuations may rarely be significant and may alternately help or hurt participants, but this problem is eliminated when daily valuation is used.

⁍ THE DISADVANTAGES OF DAILY VALUATIONS ARE NUMEROUS

The disadvantages of daily valuations include:

1. Higher cost in most cases
2. Greater difficulty in solving problems
3. Greater chance of incorrect investment decisions
4. Inability to play the float by companies
5. Less emphasis on compliance and consulting

Higher Cost

For plans of any size, daily valuation is more expensive to administer than traditional quarterly valuation, because there is simply more work involved. As an extremely general rule, daily valuation, compared to quarterly valuation, increases annual costs by 1% of assets.

The Causes of the Higher Cost   Daily valuation creates the "mood of Wall Street" in what has traditionally been the quiet backwater of pension administration. If a participant calls to request an investment change, this creates an immediate potential liability, until the money is moved by the next day. If for any reason, the request slips through the cracks and the transfer does not occur, the participant may suffer a financial loss or an opportunity cost that the administrator or the plan sponsor must make up. When a major market move occurs, as in April 1994, for example, administrators offering daily valuations can be swamped with calls from participants, and the stage is set for possible errors.

There is a second cause of daily valuation's higher cost. With daily valuation, the entire client base of an administrator is adjusted every business day. Software and hardware systems are hardly trouble-free. Any problem that might contaminate the system contaminates every single 401(k) plan in the administrator's database—not just the plans being worked on at that time. As a result, some administrators offering daily valuations adopt the axiom "If anything can go wrong, it will." They work on only one plan at a time rather than downloading daily mutual fund prices into all account files in a single operation. This limits the potential for contaminating all plans if a problem arises. However, it takes much more time.

Passing Through the Higher Costs Most plans pass these additional costs on to employees, because the pass-through of this expense rarely surfaces as an issue. Even if it does, most employees would probably elect to pay the added expense and have daily valuation anyway, because of its popularity. The costly impact of expenses charged against earnings is rarely understood by rank-and-file employees. But this will be changing as the financial press hammers away at this particular point. An article in *Forbes* entitled, "The House Take" was subtitled, "Why is running mutual funds so outlandishly profitable? Blame the public which doesn't seem to care about management fees."[1] This article is not talking specifically about daily valuation, but it illustrates the point that the public is not always concerned about the costs of anything having to do with keeping track of their money.

This, then, is an area in which the conscience and financial sophistication of the plan sponsor performs a valuable service in making the right decision in behalf of employees.

Making Daily Valuation Work in Small Companies Making the right decision about daily valuation is perhaps even more important for the plan sponsor in a small company. Daily valuation, in many ways, requires the same amount of time for a small plan as for a large plan. In a small 50-participant plan, there might typically be only one or two investment changes requested during a quarter, but all 50 accounts must be updated daily. Small plans do not have enough assets to cover the costs of these fixed, per-plan charges. A very general rule of thumb is that administrators cannot cost-effectively offer daily valuation to companies with fewer than 150–200 employees.

Until now, the discussion about daily valuation has assumed a third-party administrator offering an unlimited selection of mutual funds to the plan sponsor. In some cases, a mutual fund family will offer daily valuation to an administrator in a cost-effective package, if the administrator uses only the mutual fund company's funds. However, when a plan locks itself into one fund family, it may be setting itself up for an opportunity cost: substandard performance by that family of funds. This opportunity cost can offset any savings from the package.

Employees in small companies may be better served if the extra money that would have paid for daily valuation were spent on a larger matching contribution.

More Difficult-to-Solve Problems

Quarterly valuation is reasonably forgiving if mistakes have been made. The pool of money can be adjusted and corrected before employees are given statements. Thus, administrators and plan sponsors have a certain latitude. In contrast, daily valuation is very unforgiving: when it's bad, it's very bad. If a mistake is made, there is no pool of money to massage. The mistake has already been reflected in every participant's account. Often the mistake may be in one account and can't be found without reviewing every single account. For the administrator handling five hundred 401(k) plans and 25,000 participants, it's like having to balance 25,000 checking accounts to find a mistake in one account.

For example, the *Wall Street Journal* had a front-page article (23 June 1994) entitled "Deliberate Mispricing at Fidelity Highlights Lax Controls on Quotes."[2] A mispriced mutual fund in a daily-valued system affects the value of the participants' accounts and, thus, the amount of potential loans, termination distributions, or investment changes occurring that day. To correct the affected accounts is obviously expensive and time-consuming—yet, it must be done. In quarterly-valued systems, however, any mid-quarter glitches can be corrected before participant reports are mailed.

In the same vein, a client of mine once sent to the Janus fund a check with an account number on the check for his own internal recordkeeping. The number happened to have the same number of digits as the accounts used by Janus, and the check ended up in the Janus account of a doctor in Denver, Colorado. A daily-valued system would have instantly misallocated this amount, making the mistake public. In a quarterly-valued system, the mistake would have been quietly corrected.

Another plan sponsor made the mistake of issuing two checks for its year-end matching contribution, which doubled the contribution amount. By the time the mistake was discovered, hundreds of employees had received their share of an extra $300,000, and the extra contribution had experienced gains or losses, depending on each participant's investment choices—including investment changes. Sorting through thousands of accounts to back out the $300,000 plus its gains and losses was an expensive accounting nightmare.

Because fixing the problem in a plan with daily valuation will be expensive, problem solving often degenerates into an exercise of assigning blame. All scheduled fees charged for plan administration assume that everything is running smoothly. If the plan sponsor does something incorrectly, the administrator is reluctant to allocate the time to correct the problem, unless paid an additional fee. A troubled daily valuation plan can be very costly to put back on its feet, and it is often the plan sponsor who gets stuck footing that bill.

Greater Chance of Incorrect Investment Decisions

Daily valuation provides participants with greater flexibility to change investments, but moving money at any sign of bad economic news can produce incorrect investment decisions and poor performance.

The average investor who tries to time the market almost always ends up worse off than if a buy-and-hold strategy had been used. The crash of October 19, 1987 is an excellent example: when investors bailed out of the equities markets during the three days when the market lost about 20%, they also lost out on the subsequent gains that brought equity accounts back to almost even by December 31.

As a general rule, the average layperson trying to time the market is usually going the wrong way when changing investment mix. And, daily valuations provide participants greater opportunity to guess wrong.

No More Playing the Float

Some plan sponsors enjoy the luxury of depositing participant contributions a week or so after the money has been deducted from checks. In some cases, they may wait a month. (Employers by law have as long as 90 days to deposit funds.)

With a plan that is valued daily, the luxury of playing the float for a few weeks disappears. When participants call to get their account balances, they know immediately if deducted funds have been deposited.

Less Emphasis on Compliance and Consulting

Administration firms that offer daily valuation become so preoccupied with reporting account balances that they do not focus sufficiently on compliance and consulting issues. Their attitude becomes, "Hey, daily valuations are so popular with employees that we don't have to baby-sit the clients anymore. They will do whatever it takes, including some of what we used to do, to make this new daily valuation work for their people." And if this administration firm is two time zones away, the plan sponsor, in many cases, must hire local consultants (like lawyers who are ERISA specialists) to solve problems that the local administrator used to address.

For example, a major mutual fund organization is often criticized for not clearly stating that the client is responsible for many compliance issues that were handled by a more traditional administrator. The transmission of payroll information to this fund organization is also less forgiving. It has an "our way or the highway" mentality, and employers who are used to a more user-friendly, hand-holding approach are usually disappointed in this aspect of these daily valuation programs.

Also, the purpose of inbound money is often not monitored carefully enough. A contribution into the participant's account can be for one of three reasons: 1) the basic voluntary contribution; 2) the employer matching contribution; or 3) a loan repayment. Each source of money must be identified; but, all too often, the money is just deposited. Identifying each source of funds and balancing it becomes another expensive nightmare when it comes time to file and audit the annual form 5500 for the plan.

This different attitude toward compliance and consulting by administrators who use quarterly and daily valuations reflects a fundamental difference in their knowledge of how pension plans work and what is important.

Traditional administrators are usually trying to pass a series of exams sponsored by the American Society of Pension Actuaries. They appreciate the seriousness of compliance issues, and they have developed the ability to anticipate potential problems. Because the recordkeeping with quarterly valuations is easier and more forgiving than that of daily valuations, these administrators have the time and the emotional energy to think about more than just generating statements.

Administrators who offer daily valuation, by comparison, are paid to maintain daily balances, and they allocate less time and money to compliance. This brings us back to why many fund organizations, for example, do not prepare the annual form 5500; avoiding or farming out some portion of the administration to local firms is typical of the administrators offering daily valuation, because they need to sidestep responsibility for testing the plan and balancing the accounts. This sidestep, however, only adds to the cost.

▌▌▌▌▌ A HYBRID DAILY/QUARTERLY APPROACH CAN BE COST-EFFECTIVE

As discussed earlier in this chapter, daily valuation cannot be offered cost-effectively for plans with fewer than 150–200 participants. However, there is a hybrid solution to this obstacle.

In smaller companies, daily valuation can be offered within a quarterly valuation plan by allowing participants to open an individual account at a brokerage firm, make any investments they wish at any time, and pay the additional cost of the bookkeeping. At the end of the quarter, information about their investment activity becomes part of the aggregate reporting for the plan.

This option must be offered to all participants. However, when told that the annual bookkeeping cost is, say, $500, most participants will remain with the mutual funds chosen for the plan. But, a participant with a large account balance may find a $500 fee to be an acceptable cost for the additional flexibility, and possibly higher earnings, of investment options beyond those offered. This option adds not just daily valuation but a wider investment selection.

This hybrid approach offers an opportunity to choose from any mutual fund or even any individual stock and bond. The only caveat is that the opportunity has to be offered to *all* eligible employees. From a practical standpoint, however, most will opt for the "free" selection of mutual funds, rather than pay $500 per year for more flexibility.

A second hybrid approach values a quarterly plan every month. This generates more precise accounting for payouts and transfers. No testing is conducted, nor are employee statements generated. This is a cost-effective alternative that combats one of the major criticisms of quarterly valuations—imprecise account balances due to relatively infrequent balancing. This approach will still be less expensive and offer more investment flexibility than most daily valuation programs.

▌▌ SUMMARY

These days, whether daily valuation is worth the additional hard- and soft-dollar expense is the engine that drives the selection of vendors. In many ways, this choice may be analogous to the choice in buying an automobile: do we buy one with an automatic transmission or a stick shift? Automatics have been around for almost 50 years, but many buyers today still prefer a stick. It's more fuel efficient, and it allows the driver to push-start the car if the battery dies. In other words, the stick shift is cheaper, and it offers a simple solution to a car that won't start. This metaphor may explain why traditional quarterly 401(k) plans will not be eclipsed by daily valuation.

Daily valuation and quarterly valuation provide two very distinct ways to "keep score" in a 401(k) plan.

Administrators Using Quarterly Valuation Organize Everything by Client Company

- The money in each investment is pooled in the name of the company's 401(k) plan.
- At the end of the quarter, contributions and gains or losses are allocated to the individual participants.

Administrators Using Daily Valuation Organize Everything by Individual Participant

- Contributions and gains or losses in each investment are allocated to each participant daily.
- At the end of the quarter, the accounts of the individual participants are aggregated in the name of their respective companies.

Daily Valuation Offers Popularity and Accuracy

- Employees can track their contributions and investment gains or losses daily, and can immediately be paid their account balances upon termination of their participation in the plan.
- Changes in investment values during the quarter are more accurately allocated.

Daily Valuation Involves More Cost and Difficulty

- Daily valuation requires more administrative work and is usually not cost-effective for plans with fewer than 150–200 participants.

- Solving problems is more difficult, and the standard fees for daily valuation usually do not include solving problems.

- The ability to change investments quickly can promote hasty and incorrect investment decisions.

- Plan sponsors must deposit participant contributions more quickly.

- Administrators offering daily valuation focus on recordkeeping rather than on detecting and solving problems, and usually transfer the compliance and consulting tasks to the plan sponsor or to a local administrator.

A Hybrid Daily/Quarterly Valuation Can Work for Small Companies

- All participants are offered a wider array of investment choices, if they pay the extra cost of recordkeeping.

- The relatively few participants interested in daily valuation can be serviced at a lower cost than if the entire plan were valued daily.

- A plan concerned about inequities created by quarterly valuations can consider paying for monthly valuations.

Notes

[1] Neil Weinberg, "The House Take," *Forbes*, (4 July 1994), p. 151.
[2] McGough, R., Emshwiller, J.R., Calian, S., "Mutual Muddle: Deliberate Mispricing at Fidelity Highlights Lax Controls on Quotes," *Wall Street Journal*, (23 June 1994), p. 1.

Chapter 8

Why Vendor Selection Is Important and Difficult

So far, Part One of this book has been discussing how 401(k) plans work, and how to design and promote these plans. Before beginning Part Two, which will discuss how to select the administrators, investment managers, and other vendors who will help design and maintain the plan, the decision-maker must understand the following.

1. These selections are important because 401(k) plan administration is complicated, is subject to intricate government regulation, and requires people—not just software.

2. The selection process is difficult because 401(k) plans attract the marketing representatives of a wide array of vendors.

While this chapter deals with 401(k) plan complications that are discouraging to have to think about, these should not be viewed as reasons for not installing what will be a very popular plan and a valuable company benefit. This chapter is meant to alert the senses to problems lying just below the surface of what may be described by marketing people as "a real simple 401(k) plan that will be no problem." It's like when my 16-year-old son started to veer into oncoming traffic while fiddling with my car's air conditioning: I yelled just in time, and he learned the valuable lesson that you can't take your eyes off the road, even for a second. His enthusiasm for driving remains undiminished. He just appreciates the dangers better. This chapter should be viewed in the same light, because the rest of the book helps you put together a 401(k) plan that really will be "no problem."

ⅢⅢ 401(k) PLANS ARE COMPLICATED AND HEAVILY REGULATED

First, understand that 401(k) plans are complicated. Unlike a conventional pension plan having one contribution per year and annual accounting, 401(k) plans involve contributions each pay period, loans to participants, changes in investment choices, and other transactions by individual participants who can make unilateral decisions about their accounts.

Operating a 401(k) plan is much more akin to running a local credit union. However, because it is a pension plan, its operations must adhere strictly to the complicated matrix of IRS and Labor Department laws that prevent these plans from favoring highly compensated employees. The price of operating the plan in violation of these laws is the entire plan's disqualification; this triggers the loss of the corporate tax deduction for all money contributed and many other problems and penalties. Since none of the penalties are even tax-deductible, the cost of a problem can be huge. This threat of potential disqualification very effectively encourages plan sponsors and administrators to adhere to the exacting standards of the 401(k) regulations; a few case histories can illustrate this. For the record, the IRS disqualified roughly 150 pension plans in 1993.

Turning $20,000 Mistakes into $150,000 Problems

Earlier chapters discussed how a company can exclude certain of its employees from participation in the 401(k) plan and how any employees not specifically excluded are automatically included in the plan for purposes of testing. The first case history shows what happens when a 401(k) plan does not meet these rules.

A large farming company had not included some of its employees in the 401(k) plan, and did not specifically exclude them in the trust document. According to the pension laws, the farming company had discriminated against these workers.

The starting point for correcting the problem was to calculate what the excluded employees would have contributed to the plan if they had contributed the same percentage of their pay as had the average non–highly compensated employees. This amount totalled $20,000.

The plan sponsor would have been happy to have contributed this amount to the plan to solve the problem. He expected to pay some penalties and interest, so that the total cost to fix the problem and move on was expected to be $20,000 to $30,000.

The IRS began the discussion by presenting a bill for $800,000! This amount represented the taxes and penalties on contributions from all plan's participants, because the entire plan was disqualified. Obviously, there was a lot of light between $20,000 and $800,000; but technically, the IRS had every legal right to collect this $800,000.

The final settlement was $150,000; a $20,000 mistake cost $150,000 to correct.

The plan administrator was not at fault because the client had prepared all of the employee information and had just arbitrarily decided to exclude some employees from the census information submitted to the administrator. This is an easy mistake to make. Plan sponsors sometimes slide into a habit of providing information on only employees who participate in the plan, or they fail to add data for a newly acquired company. For example, the company owner may make a personal investment in a winery, and no one considers that, because of "controlled group of companies" regulations, the winery's employees are now part of the original company and must be brought into the plan.

Controlled Group Rules Illustrate Pension Plan Complexity Any decision-maker having trouble appreciating the complexity of pension regulations need only read the "regs" outlining what is a controlled group. In part, these regs read as follows:

> A controlled group of Corporations exists where there is (1) a parent-subsidiary group of corporations connected through at least 80% stock ownership, or (2) a "brother-sister" controlled group in which (a) five or fewer people own 80% or more of the stock value or voting power of each corporation, and (b) the same five or fewer people together own more than 50% of the value of the voting stock of each corporation, taking into account the ownership of each person only to the extent such ownership is identical with respect to each organization. [Ref, Int. Rev. Code 1563(a)]

I think we will all agree that the citation above is so convoluted that it could be grist for the mill of a standup comic at the next pension convention. However, administrators and ERISA attorneys are called upon to interpret the laws that are applicable in many multiple-company situations, and the potential disqualification of a plan hangs on the balance.

Beyond the "controlled group" laws, there are even more

stringent laws referring to "affiliated service groups" and "affiliated management groups." These are situations in which companies that are *simply doing business with each other* can be construed to be part of a controlled group and effectively required to have one pension plan covering all.

The Million Dollar Signatures

To protect the rights of participants and spouses, before money in a 401(k) account is distributed, a series of documents must be signed by both participant and spouse, and the signatures may not be more than 90 days old when the distribution is finally made. If this sounds like a lot of work, it is.

But in 1993, a major company that chose not to bother with this documentation was fined over one million dollars. The firm simply sent checks for the distribution amount without processing the required distribution paperwork.

The $100-a-Day Lapse

Employees have a right to receive copies of plan documents that relate in any way to their account balances. For instance, if participants who are terminating their involvement in the plan question how their vested account balance was calculated, they have the right to see all plan documents that describe how that calculation was made. If a plan sponsor fails to respond to that request, the penalty can be $100 per day.

So, here's a classic example of an unnecessary expense: a plan sponsor pays the correct vested account balance to a participant, but because of arrogance or just plain laziness, fails to send the requested documents for about four months; the plan sponsor can be liable for (at $100 per day) a $12,000 penalty. The IRS is forcing employers to pay these penalties; they cannot be paid as an expense of the plan.

Plan Sponsors Cannot Escape Their Responsibilities

The power of the IRS to penalize is commensurate with the potential for abuse of these plans. They offer substantial tax savings for company owners and key managers at the possible expense of lower-paid employees. Because these plans are largely self-policed and because they are complicated, the natural temptation would be to avoid being compulsive about complying with the law. To "encourage" compliance, the IRS adopts the strategy of Teddy Roosevelt, "Speak softly and carry a big stick."

In a way, this draconian approach is analogous to the policy adopted by the Drug Enforcement Agency when it seizes an entire piece of property after finding a small plot of marijuana in the backyard. This explains why most of the remaining dope growers in Northern California grow their pot on other people's property, like government or lumber-company land.

For pension plan sponsors, there is no comparable opportunity to "park" owners and employees in someone else's 401(k) plan. So-called "employee leasing companies," which were in vogue for a few years, were about the only option plan sponsors could use to slough off their responsibilities. Changes in the tax laws have largely closed that loophole.

Neither can plan sponsors escape responsibility by using a major financial institution as the plan's administrator; these institutions can use many techniques to shirk responsibility without appearing to do so. For example, a major brokerage firm has added to its plan document—in extremely small print—the note that the document is "not guaranteed to comply with TEFRA, DEFRA, and REA." What plan sponsor could be expected to know what that small notation refers to? In fact, it is saying that the plan document may not comply with the three recent tax law changes and that the brokerage firm is taking no responsibility for making sure that it does! The IRS is now focusing on these plans administered by what they call the "asset chasers." The next round of IRS audits is expected to unearth a goldmine of disqualified plans for the Federal government.

Another pitfall to watch out for: plan documents are often left unsigned, even though they have been prepared. *A plan with no signed trust document is disqualified.* This is often a danger with major financial institutions (whose primary objective is selling investments), because they are not submitting a client's plan document to the IRS for approval. Instead, they have gained approval for a "cookie cutter" plan document that can be used in *almost* any situation. The operative word here is "almost." Sometimes, a plan document must be customized to meet a specific situation, and when financial institutions are obsessed with getting the money under management, they often overlook basic compliance issues. To their credit, many investment companies are at least honest about it; they refuse to prepare the form 5500 for the plan and, thus, do not take any responsibility for the testing.

Compliance issues, then, are often the Achilles' heel of a

401(k) plan. A plan sponsor can select great investments and what appears to be a reasonably priced administrator, but if the plan is disqualified or if the administrator can't anticipate and solve problems, mistakes can trigger stratospheric costs that are way out of proportion to the dollars involved in the mistake itself.

IIIII 401(k) PLAN ADMINISTRATION REQUIRES PEOPLE—NOT JUST SOFTWARE

All too often, plan sponsors expect their 401(k) administration to be run like their payroll service or their health plans. We're all conditioned to think that if something is computerized, it is basically bullet-proof, unless incorrect data has been entered. But less than 50% of 401(k) plan administration has been computerized. As plan sponsors struggle to stay on top of one of their most popular employee benefits, they must remember this fundamental: administration involves judgement calls and the ability to provide reasoned advice based on experience. Administration requires people—not just software.

The plan sponsor's goal is thus to create the perfect marriage between the plan and the administrator, investment manager, or other vendor. Plan sponsors must first identify their plan's greatest need and then pick the vendor accordingly. Three simple examples will illustrate this point.

First, employees in an engineering company are analytical and self-styled investment experts. They may demand a wide variety of investment selections, and quickly criticize investment selections that lack excellent past performance. As a pension consultant in cases like this, I generally avoid recommending a packaged selection of investments offered by a financial institution because it does not provide the greatest possible investment flexibility.

Second, a law partnership, by comparison, will be primarily concerned with compliance and the intricate year-end calculation that determines each partner's contribution to the plan. The average plan offered by a financial institution will not have people equipped to help with these calculations. The job will fall to the partners themselves and their CPA.

Third, a large company will be well served by a plan offered by a financial institution because the average employee in a less-personal environment will be happier with a plan that offers daily valuations and an 800 phone number they can call for account information. They will rarely be aware, however, of the additional cost they bear for that level of reporting and flexibility.

Choosing the right combination of vendors, then, begins with an appreciation of the potential problems that plans can have because of their complexity and their need to comply with government requirements. The key is for the plan sponsor to identify the problems that could occur more readily in his or her company and then choose the vendor combination best equipped to thwart those problems.

IIIII THERE IS A HUGE CHOICE OF VENDORS

Selecting the right vendor combination can be difficult because of the huge number of vendors and the barrage of marketing people and material to which the plan sponsor is subjected.

In a typical situation, a company has a pension plan that started out years ago as a simple profit-sharing plan with minimal amounts of money contributed. Then, the company added the 401(k) provision, and employees jumped at the opportunity to deposit pre-tax dollars. Now, after several years, the plan has about $500,000 in assets, and it has attracted the attention of the investment and insurance marketing organizations, because all pension plan information is public. Anyone can buy lists arranged by zip code that tell the type of pension plan, the plan sponsor, the amount of money, the number of participants, and even the name of the plan contact person. This explains why we receive so many cold calls from vendors selling 401(k) plan services.

As the plan sponsor listens to sales people, he or she hears a lot of talk about one-stop shopping, daily valuation, electronic data transfer, and plenty of other hot concepts that sound great. They are great. The question is, do they actually work in practice and are they reasonably priced?

The bewildering array of resources available for maintaining a 401(k) plan are often complicated to analyze from a cost-benefit standpoint because the tasks are so diverse, and their actual costs are often not fully divulged or easily determined.

As we will see in Part Two, the exercise of choosing vendors to assist in the operation of the plan involves an assessment of their ability and cost. No single organization offers optimal performance in investment management and administration, so piecing together the 401(k) plan becomes a study in the art of compromise.

‖‖

SUMMARY

The importance of the administrators, investment managers, and other vendors selected for the 401(k) plan cannot be overestimated. In preparation for Part Two's discussion about the selection process, plan sponsors must realize the importance of these decisions.

401(k) Plans Require Intensive and Competent Management

- Plans are complicated because of the large number of transactions.
- Plans are heavily regulated by the government.

401(k) Plans Must Scrupulously Comply with Government Regulations

- The regulations are complex and rely on the plan to police itself.
- The penalties if the regulations are not met are extremely severe as well as disproportionate to the actual mistake.
- The plan sponsor cannot escape responsibility for compliance.

The Choice of 401(k) Plan Vendors Is Huge and Can Be Confusing

- Pension plan information is public, and the decision-maker is usually the target of swarms of marketing people.
- Assessing the benefits and costs of the various ways to have a plan administered and its investments managed is difficult.

PART TWO

TASKS, VENDORS, AND COSTS

Part Two of this book discusses

- **The tasks and costs of administration and investment management**

- **The ways that administration and investment management can be performed, and the advantages and disadvantages of each approach**

- **The audit and legal functions required in a 401(k) plan**

Chapter 9

Administration and Investment Management Tasks

My doctor once referred to the "Dermatologist Syndrome." People with skin problems are rarely satisfied with the results they receive from the first dermatologist they see, so after a few weeks of treatment they move to a different dermatologist. The cycle continues until, about five dermatologists later, they find themselves back at their first dermatologist. By this time, the skin problem has pretty much gone away by itself.

The Dermatologist Syndrome is often seen in the 401(k) environment, where disappointed plan sponsors keep struggling to find the perfect plan. When the process is applied to 401(k) plans, however, the churning of investment managers and administrators can cost everyone—plan sponsor and participants—an unconscionable amount of money.

To help the plan sponsor select administrators and investment managers, this chapter discusses the tasks that they perform and the importance of these tasks.

ⅠⅠⅠⅠⅠ ADMINISTRATION IS THE NUTS AND BOLTS OF OPERATING A PLAN

In selecting administrators, the plan sponsor must understand the tasks for which the administrators are being hired:

1. Complying with government regulations
2. Consulting on changes in plan design
3. Record-keeping for individual participant accounts
4. Communicating investment information to participants

Any problems in the performance of these tasks will likely be detected first in-house, and so the plan sponsor must also understand the importance of the in-house contact person.

Complying with Government Regulations

To preserve its tax-qualified status, the 401(k) plan must comply with all testing and reporting requirements, as discussed in earlier chapters.

Every aspect of a 401(k) plan must be done correctly. However, mistakes in some areas can be corrected more easily than in others. Accounting mistakes, for example, embarrass everyone responsible, but they can be corrected relatively easily. And a mutual fund that has substandard performance can simply be replaced.

Compliance problems, however, can be a nightmare. Failing a discrimination test and not correcting it by the end of the following year can jeopardize the tax-qualification of the entire plan and also trigger substantial penalties payable by the company sponsoring the plan.

And the IRS is auditing 401(k) plans more frequently. For most of the late 1980s, the "feeding trough" of IRS pension plan auditors was the overfunded and abused defined-benefit pension plans enjoyed for years by doctors and dentists. Having milked that resource dry, the government began to aim its guns at 401(k) plans in 1990. The IRS has increased by a factor of five the number of agents assigned to audit 401(k) plans, and is generally focusing on those plans with more than $1,000,000 in assets.

Compliance, then, is that all-powerful "invisible shield" that needs constant attention during the operation of a 401(k) plan.

Consulting on Changes in Plan Design

Chapter 5 discussed the initial consulting that helps a company decide what type of 401(k) plan best suits its situation, based on the demographics of the work force and the compensation philosophy of the company.

Consulting is also needed after the plan is underway, because continual changes in the work force or the tax laws can require a "massaging" of some of the plan's basic components.

These simple design changes can be the most cost-effective way to solve, for example, a testing problem. Yet, ongoing consulting is often the weak link in many plans that emphasize investment selection or generating participant statements on time.

In addition, many plan sponsors focus on the out-of-pocket expense to maintain their 401(k) plans; but, the biggest expense is often the opportunity cost of a plan that could accomplish much more for the same administrative fees. Some of the best money spent to administer a plan may be the few extra dollars spent to review that design.

Record Keeping for Individual Participant Accounts

Record keeping links the individual participant's account to the pooled investment selections.

The individual contributions to 401(k) plans are pooled and allocated to the investments (the mutual funds usually) offered by the plan and selected by the participants. The mutual fund company keeps no record of any individual participant; instead, for each 401(k) plan, there is a single investor, say, the "ABC Inc. 401(k) Retirement Trust."

The administrator divides the pool of money in each mutual fund into individual accounts and allocates to each participant his or her share of earnings, gains, or losses. The administrator then prepares reports each quarter that summarize the activity in each participant's account.

Communicating Investment Information to Participants

Employee communication first educates the participant about the plan (how it operates, the tax savings, the loan provisions, the options upon termination of employment, etc.), and second, educates the participant about investments so that informed decisions can be made.

During the first few years of a 401(k) plan, communication should emphasize how the plan operates. Investment information should be almost incidental, because the participants' account balances are relatively small. As these balances grow, participants will need to know more about investments. For many participants, the $10,000 in their account may be far and away the most money they have ever saved. Short of winning the lottery, nothing triggers a thirst for investment knowledge more effectively than an ever-growing 401(k) account balance.

The In-House Contact Person

A Greek philosopher (Plato, I think) once said, "the smartest people in your legal system should be your policemen, because they are at the point where most justice takes place." By analogy, many problems with 401(k) plans are first discovered and corrected in-house. The contact person at the company sponsoring the plan must be detail- and numbers-oriented.

The contact person must also be interested in the 401(k) plan and want it to succeed. If the plan is viewed as a necessary evil at worst and a nuisance at best, the contact person will find solving problems to be unnecessarily difficult, and may indulge in finger pointing when problems arise.

And these problems are not necessarily anyone's fault. Reasonable, intelligent, hard-working people can now and then miss details—details that can change the entire accounting or ADP Test results of a plan. Surveys now show that the single most aggravating problem experienced by human resource professionals centers on the ongoing demands of their 401(k) plans. With the right synergy, your plan need not be part of this statistic.

Decision-makers must be aware of the tradeoff between the quality of the in-house contact person and the administrator. Today, administration companies are under pressure to keep fees competitive and still offer flawless service. Yet, the plan can not be administered by clerical personnel no matter how computerized an administration company may be. These plans demand people at all levels who can think and solve problems. The least expensive administration usually means substandard service and expensive problems sooner or later. Yet, inexpensive administration offers hard-dollar savings. Many decision-makers will choose the savings today and hope that they have reasonable luck and no future problems. When adopting this latter approach, having an experienced, intelligent in-house 401(k) contact person is imperative.

Basically, the contact person should understand how payroll systems work, because much of their responsibility will involve payroll deductions and changes. They should also understand some of the basic rules of testing so that they can anticipate situations where testing will be a problem. Virtually all administrators have employee manuals that they provide at the outset of their relationship. These manuals usually offer comprehensive information about the operation of the plan.

Plan Sponsor magazine is a good resource, as is *The 401(k) Plan Answer Book* for those wanting more information. *Tax Facts,401(k) Advisor,* and *Pension Benefits* are also user-friendly resources, providing answers to common questions that arise during the operation of a 401(k) plan.[1]

Without both good administrators and employer contact people, a 401(k) will be paddling upstream in its efforts to succeed.

||||| INVESTMENT MANAGEMENT IS MORE IMPORTANT THAN EVER

There are two levels of investment management:

1. Investment advice
2. Money management

Investment advice involves selecting the mutual funds that will be offered to plan participants. (In almost all 401(k) plans, the investments selected are mutual funds because their format accommodates the many small transactions for individual participants that are part of the normal operation of 401(k) plans.) Plan sponsors can be their own investment advisors and select mutual funds using information in publications and mutual fund rating services. Or, plan sponsors can hire outside firms or individuals to help select the funds to be offered. Chapter 13 discusses the mutual fund selection process.

Money management involves the buying and selling of stocks and/or bonds, and keeping track on a minute-by-minute basis of every transaction. These functions are performed by the mutual funds selected as investment choices for the plan.

Money management and investment advice is becoming increasingly important as:

1. Employees have larger account balances and are demanding better investment performance
2. Section 404(c) regulations suggest more attention be paid to investments

Because many plans have operated for eight years or longer, participants now have substantial account balances, and they are more concerned about investment management. Participants increasingly accost the average CFO or human resources professional at the watercooler with questions regarding investment returns, or the lack of them.

New Section 404(c) Regulations

Another reason for the increased importance of investment management has been passage of final regulations under Section 404(c) of the Department of Labor Code. These regulations, effective January 1, 1994, stipulate that:

1. Participants in a 401(k) plan should be given account balance statements at least quarterly.

2. Participants should be able to choose from three investment types with different characteristics of risk and return: a guaranteed investment, a balanced fund, and a growth fund.

3. The plan committee or trustees should review the investments at least annually and measure them against standards of comparison for each investment category.

4. Each investment should have a written statement of objectives. (Virtually every mutual fund sold today has its objective expressed in the prospectus, so plans using mutual funds automatically meet this provision.)

Contrary to popular belief, Section 404(c) is not a law; it is simply a guideline. But if its provisions are met and a participant, disgruntled because of investment performance, sues the plan, the plan sponsor's liability is limited.

To date, lawsuits like this have been rare. More common are lawsuits against plans for producing extremely late participant statements that lead to losses or opportunity costs because the participants were unable to change investments within a reasonable time frame. In the future, however, the potential for lawsuits will increase, as account balances increase and attorneys can take these cases on a contingency basis; a new subset of the legal profession will arise.

While Section 404(c) calls for provisions that plans should offer anyway and that probably 95% of all 401(k) plans *do* offer, these provisions add an additional imperative beyond just common sense. They have focused more attention on investments, and plan sponsors must realize that selecting investments goes beyond their own personal interests.

Section 404(c) is viewed by some as "The Stock Brokers' and Financial Planners' Relief Act of 1994," as plan sponsors start paying for help in "complying" with the new regulation. However, there are cost-effective ways to meet its requirements. As with hiring any outside firm, the keys are to control how the firm is used and its cost.

IIIIIIIIIIIIIIIIIIIIIIIIIIIIIIIIIIIIIIIIIIIIIIIIIIIIIIIIIIIIIIIIIIIIIIIIIIIIIII
SUMMARY

If administration is a science, then investment management is an art. Administration involves accounting and legal functions. Administrators satisfy the client with speed, correct results, and plan operation that complies with IRS demands.

By comparison, investment management involves the two-step process of first choosing a good investment advisor who will, in turn, help you decide on a selection of money managers (mutual funds) to offer as investment choices for your plan.

In some cases, the plan sponsor may act as his or her own investment advisor and choose the mutual fund offerings without any help. This is legal, but may not be wise.

In selecting outside firms and an in-house contact person, plan sponsors must understand the tasks they do and the importance of these tasks.

401(k) Plans Must Comply with Government Regulations

- Penalties for non-compliance are severe.
- IRS audits are increasingly frequent.

The 401(k) Plan Design Process Is Ongoing

- Changes in the work force and tax laws may require changes in the design of the plan.
- Engaging a design consultant can be the most cost-effective way to solve problems.

Record Keeping Links the Participant with the Plan's Pooled Assets

- Record keeping translates the aggregate assets of the plan into individual participant accounts.
- Timely statements are vital to participant satisfaction.

Communication Educates Participants About the Plan and About Investing

- In the plan's early years, communication should educate participants about how the plan operates.
- After account balances become significant, communication should educate participants about investing.

The In-House Contact Person Is the First Line of Defense

- Most problems are detected and solved in-house.
- The in-house contact person must be able to think and solve problems.
- The in-house contact person becomes more important if a less qualified, but lower cost, administrator is selected.

Investment Management Consists of Money Management and Investment Advice

- The plan sponsors, using various sources of investment advice (usually investment advisors), select the mutual funds or other money managers.
- A money manager, usually a mutual fund, invests the plan's assets in the underlying stocks and bonds that comprise the mutual fund's assets.

Investment Management Is Now More Important Than Ever

- Larger account balances make participants more interested in investment results.
- Section 404(c), which recommends methods for handling investments, is focusing more attention on investment management.

Note

[1] *Plan Sponsor* is published ten times a year by Asset International, Greenwich, CT. *The 401(k) Plan Answer Book,* by Joan Gucciardi, Steven J. Franz, Joan C. McDonagh, and John Michael Maier, is published by Panel Publishers, Inc., New York. *Tax Facts* is published by The National Underwriter Company, Cincinnati, OH. *401(k) Advisor* and *Pension Benefits* are published by Panel Publishers (a division of Aspen Publishers, Inc.), New York.

Chapter 10

Administration and Investment Management Costs

Chapter 9 discussed the administration and investment management tasks in a 401(k) plan. Cost is a major factor in selecting firms to perform these tasks. And analyzing the costs that each firm proposes to charge is difficult because these costs are often disguised or hidden.

This chapter discusses the different types of administration and investment management costs. Chapter 11 then presents plan sponsors with a method of fairly comparing competing proposals.

IIIII ADMINISTRATION COSTS *SEEM* STRAIGHTFORWARD

Any comparison of administration costs should be on an "apples to apples" basis. The term "administration" can have different meanings to different vendors. It *should* mean being completely responsible for IRS and Labor Department compliance, recommending ongoing changes in plan design, keeping records for all plan transactions and producing employee statements, preparing the form 5500, and assuring that an Errors and Omissions or Professional Liability insurance policy is in force.

As an extremely general rule of thumb, 401(k) plan administration currently costs about $100 per year per participant. Access Research, a market research firm in Windsor, Connecticut, says that annual recordkeeping and administrative fees average more than $100 per employee for plans with fewer than 100 employees but drop to $23 per employee for plans with more than 5,000 employees.[1] Since the vast majority of U.S. employees work for companies with fewer than 500 employees, it's safe to assume $100 as a reasonable cost in most situations.

There may be other administration costs for participant loans, termination payouts, and the annual CPA audit for plans with over 100 employees. As discussed in Chapter 4, loan costs should be and are almost always borne by the participant who borrows: $75–$100 to set up the loan, $50 per year to administer it, and $200 if collateral is involved. The CPA audit, when required, will cost whatever the company's CPA firm charges, regardless of which 401(k) program is chosen. In most cases, these other administration costs, even if substantial, will be the same across the board and do not play a large role in cost comparisons between different 401(k) programs.

In addition to the hard-dollar costs of administration, there is a soft-dollar cost related to the quality of the administrator. In the small pension plan business, there are so-called "dirty dish" and "clean dish" administrators. Clean dish administrators wash dishes whenever a dish is dirty; i.e., they keep their plans trouble-free and are hired to clean up other plans. Dirty dish administrators wash dishes only when a clean dish is needed; i.e., they do the least possible work, but they work for below-market fees. They tolerate a certain loss of clients, and because their fees are so competitive, they always have plenty of new, unsuspecting clients. However, sooner or later, their substandard work becomes the liability of their clients and an expensive repair job for the next pension administrator.

As an example of a soft-dollar administration cost, assume that a plan sponsor is paying $6,000 annually for administration. But because the administration is substandard, there is a 10% chance that the plan will have a problem that costs $50,000 to fix; there is, statistically, an additional soft-dollar cost of $5,000. The total administration cost, then, is $11,000 annually. The plan sponsor would be better off paying, say, $7,000 annually to a firm with a reputation for doing good work.

When it comes to administration, hire brain power and hard work. Plan sponsors get what they pay for—as many have found out the hard way.

Also, plan sponsors should not be fooled by a few good references. Any administration company still in business has been lucky on at least a few plans and can give those plans as references. Instead, plan sponsors should use this book to generate some questions and trust their instincts when answers are received. Make sure to meet the person who will be responsible for the plan, not just the marketing people.

IIIII INVESTMENT MANAGEMENT COST IS WHERE COMPLICATIONS ARISE

There are two layers of investment cost that correspond to the two levels of investment management:

1. Money management—The cost of investing and accounting for the money managed by mutual funds

2. Investment advice—The cost of choosing mutual funds or other money managers

The Cost of Money Management

The first layer of cost pays the money manager (for example, the load or no-load mutual fund) for selecting investments, keeping track of their investors' accounts, and conducting trades. This cost is very basic and unavoidable, because no company will manage assets for nothing.

For performing these tasks, the average mutual fund charges annually about 1.1% of the account balance, but most popular funds found in 401(k) plans seem to charge about 1%. (For money market funds, that cost is typically about 0.35% per year.)

To this 1% ongoing cost of managing the money, most plans offered by the insurance and stock brokerage industries add 1% to 1.5% annually to pay for the financial institution's marketing.

The effect of an extra 1% per year on the average highly compensated employee can be dramatic. Assume an average annual contribution of $10,000, contributed over 24 pay periods during each year. In one scenario, the contributions earn an average of 10% per year compounded, and in the second scenario, with the extra 1% marketing fee subtracted, the contributions earn 9%. In just ten years, the extra 1% has cost the executive about $10,000 of earnings and in 20 years has cost the executive about $80,000.

Remember, the magic of compound interest works against us when fees are charged against plan earnings.

The Cost of Investment Advice

The second layer of cost, for investment advice, is where confusion and bad decisions abound. Plan sponsors can be their own investment advisors and select mutual funds that meet the investment category and diversification requirements of Section 404(c). Or, they can hire an investment advisor, such as a financial planner, brokerage firm, or insurance company that will recommend mutual funds. Whether to hire investment advisors and how much to pay them are the decisions that the plan sponsor faces.

Two factors complicate the cost analysis of investment advice:

1. Commissions or fees paid for investment advice or money management may sometimes subsidize the ongoing administrative costs of the plan

2. The cost of investment advice will inevitably be split in some way between the participant and the employer.

Allocating costs between administration or investment management and between participants or employer is illustrated by the following matrix:

	Employer Paid	Participant Paid
Administration	A	B
Money Management/ Investment Advice	C	D

Box A   Box A represents a small plan in which the employer pays for administration. In most small companies, this is the norm because assets in the plan are insufficient to pay for administration. In this case, the participants would pay for money management and investment advice. A combination of boxes A and D represents the cost allocation of most small-company 401(k) plans.

Box B   Box B represents a larger plan with assets of $1,000,000 or more, which is large enough for the plan (the participants, effectively) to pay for administration.

Because administration costs are, for the most part, based on the number of participants, these costs remain fixed as the assets of the plan increase. Over time, a plan can begin paying for administration out of earnings with a minimal impact on participant results. For example, if a plan with $1,000,000 of assets earns about 10% per year (or $100,000), deducting administrative costs of $3,000 from the earnings only reduces the return from 10% to 9.7%. A combination of boxes B and D represents most 401(k)s of larger companies or of smaller companies whose plans have well over one million dollars in assets.

Box C   Box C represents a plan in which the company is paying a fee for investment advice that is independent of the investments themselves. In other words, the investment advisor is not receiving commissions but is charging the corporation a fee for investment advice: helping the owner or the plan trustees review or choose investments, continuously monitoring the performance of the funds, and helping individual participants select an investment mix. In some smaller companies whose owners have disproportionately large account balances, the company will pay all expenses of investment management because the earnings in the plan, and the owner's share of them, will be greater. A combination of boxes A and C represents the best possible deal for participants, but a combination this "pure" is rare.

Box D   Box D represents a plan in which the plan sponsor is paying for investment advice and money management in the form of fees and commissions paid directly to brokers and the mutual funds by the funds themselves. In this case, the employee-participants are essentially paying the cost, and there is no option for the employer to reimburse the plan for fees and commissions paid, even if the employer had preferred to do so. (The reason for this is explained later in the chapter.) Even no-load mutual funds have an annual fee of 1%, which is effectively paid by employees out of earnings. But in addition to this standard fee, a typical 12b-1 load mutual fund, for example, charges an annual 1% 12b-1 fee to all fund investors, and then uses the proceeds to pay brokers an up-front commission of as much as 5% as they generate new money into the fund from new investors. The term "12b-1 fee" refers to a Securities and Exchange Commission ruling that allows funds to charge existing shareholders an annual fee to compensate stockbrokers.

In many cases, there may be no clear lines between the boxes above. Costs may be shifted between administration and investment management and between the employer and participant. The plan sponsor should recognize these shifts and their importance.

Shifting Administration Costs to Investment Management

Some financial institutions provide both administration and investment management as a package. In these package plans (which will be more fully discussed in Chapter 11), the cost of investment management may be greater than normal, but this is offset by lower administration costs. Also, the plan may offer what many perceive as the additional value of daily valuations and an 800 phone number for changing investments.

Plan sponsors confronted with this type of 401(k) package plan should look carefully for where they might be paying that standard administration cost of $100 per employee and investment cost of 1% of assets. One thing is clear: the financial institution is charging that money somewhere.

Back during the famous Watergate hearings, Senator Sam Ervin kept saying, "Follow the money. That's how you can figure out what is happening here." The same can be said for 401(k) cost analysis. Using $100 per participant and 1% of assets as standards of comparison, plan sponsors can then sift through the pricing structure of a variety of proposals to determine what additional costs represent a premium price for the employer and the participants.

Shifting Employer Costs to the Participant

Who is paying for the 401(k) plan, the employer or the participants, can be confusing. Typically, plan administration is paid by the employer, and investment management is paid by the participants as an expense against the plan's earnings. However, there are no hard-and-fast rules about this traditional allocation of costs. Some 401(k) package plans allocate substantial administrative and investment management expenses to the participants, which may appear to be inexpensive to the plan sponsors. There are two reasons why it may not be inexpensive.

First, plan sponsors should realize that there is nothing magical about charging most of the costs to the plan. Any administration or management expense can be charged to the plan. And a package plan that already does it is not necessarily doing anyone a favor, especially because it is impossible to go the other way; the plan sponsor cannot reimburse the plan for expenses that are built into the mutual funds or the insurance company package plans. (Recent regulations prohibit reimbursement. It is viewed as an additional contribution to the plan that is distributed disproportionately to those participants with large account balances; it is thus discriminatory.)

A plan sponsor who wants to adopt that "paid-by-the-plan" approach should control the degree to which it is used, but many packaged plans rule out this flexibility.

Second, in smaller companies, plan sponsors often must be especially sensitive to cost allocation. If a handful of key employees have, say, one-third of the plan's assets, then they will wind up paying one-third of the costs shifted to the participants. Remember the earlier example in which an extra 1% marketing fee charged against earnings reduced an executive's earnings by $10,000 during a ten-year period. Plan sponsors who think they are getting "free" administration are in fact getting very expensive administration.

To make matters worse, they have turned what would have been a expense deductible by the company, if it had paid the fee, into an expense not deductible by the pension plan because the plan pays no taxes. A plan sponsor may have effectively doubled the administrative cost by removing its tax-deductible status. And a plan sponsor who is also a participant may have unwittingly paid a portion of the plan's costs using his or her own precious tax-deferred retirement dollars. This is sacrosanct money that not only is tax-deferred itself *but that compounds rapidly on a tax-deferred basis*.

If reasonably sophisticated businesspeople were to pick any source of money for paying a business expense, simple arithmetic would tell them that their own pension money represented the most expensive option from an opportunity-cost standpoint. For most clear-thinking and informed individuals, their 401(k) account is the last money they would ever elect to touch.

||||||||||||||||||||||||||||||||||||||||||||||||||||||||||||||||||||||||||||||
SUMMARY

Administration and investment management constitute the two basic costs of a 401(k) plan. These costs take many different forms and are often disguised or are not what they first appear to be. Before analyzing the proposals of competing administrators and investment managers, plan sponsors must clearly understand these costs.

Administration Cost *Seems* Straightforward

- For most companies, administration costs $100 per participant per year.
- In comparing the costs of plans, make sure that the plans perform comparable administrative tasks.
- Consider the soft-dollar costs of choosing less-qualified administrators.

Investment Management Cost Is Not Straightforward

- Basic money management costs 1% of assets under management per year.
- Paying more than 1% for money management can be expensive because the effect of compounding in a tax-deferred environment magnifies the lost earning from any extra fees.
- Shifting payment of investment expenses from the plan sponsor to the plan (the participants) reduces plan earnings and can adversely affect company owners and highly compensated employees who have large account balances.

Chapter 11

A Package Plan or a Team of Advisors

Chapters 9 and 10 discussed the tasks and costs of 401(k) administration and investment management. These tasks can be performed by a single firm offering a package approach or by a team of firms. This chapter presents a framework for comparing the costs of these approaches and discusses their advantages and disadvantages.

||||| THERE ARE TWO BASIC APPROACHES

Administration and investment management can be performed using two basic approaches, plus some variations on these approaches.

First, package programs perform both the investment management and the administration of the plan. These programs are offered by financial institutions such as banks, brokerage firms, mutual fund companies, and life insurance companies.

Second, a third-party administrator can design, install, and administer the plan, and one or more financial institutions can provide investment management, thus creating a team of advisors. Members of the team can be changed without changing the entire plan. For example, a mutual fund can be terminated without changing administrators, and an administrator can be terminated without changing any mutual funds.

Third-party administrators are usually independent of any financial institutions or investment services, and they are independent of the investment choices offered by the plan. These firms are paid a fee, as opposed to sales commissions or charges that reduce the plan's earnings.

Third, several hybrids of the basic two approaches exist. A third-party administrator can administer the plan and also help the plan sponsor select mutual funds, i.e., provide investment advice but not money management. Or, financial institutions can manage the plan's investments and contract with regional third-party administrators. Or, a financial institution can manage the plan's investments and use its commissions to pay for or subsidize the cost of a third-party administrator.

||||| USE THE COST COMPARISON WORKSHEET TO ANALYZE PLANS

The possible combinations of service providers presents the plan sponsor with a challenge: how to compare the costs of competing plans. The Cost Comparison Worksheet provides a framework for this analysis; it separates the plan's costs between administration and investment management and between employer-paid and participant-paid.

Defining Costs

Before illustrating the use of the worksheet, the various cost components should be understood.

Administration Cost

1. Base Annual Fee: This fee is usually a fixed dollar amount.
2. Per Participant Fee: This fee is based on the number of employees who contribute to the plan or on the number of *eligible* participants, regardless of whether they contribute to the plan.
3. Administrative Asset Fee (or fee for special services): This fee, if charged, is typically 0.2% to 1% of assets.

Investment Management Fees

1. Money Management Fee: This fee is charged against the plan's earnings (or against principal in years when an investment loses money).
2. Up-front Commission: Sales commissions are subtracted from investments in a mutual fund, but these are almost unheard of in today's 401(k) plans.

3. "Back-end" 12b-1 Fee: These fees are charged if money is removed from the mutual fund. If fund redemptions exceed deposits, a fee of as much as 7% is applied against the money withdrawn; typically, the fee reduces each year and reaches zero after seven to ten years.

   This fee is almost impossible to administer; it is usually waived for individual participants in 401(k) plans. However, 12b-1 fees are retained for the overall plan; if the plan cancels a mutual fund, the back-end fees are charged against the money withdrawn.

   Instead of the mutual fund back-end 12b-1 fee, the life insurance industry uses an "annuity wrap fee." By putting mutual funds inside an annuity (a life insurance product), the 401(k) plan can be sold by life insurance agents who might otherwise lack a securities license.

4. Annual Distribution Fee: This is a second form of 12b-1 fee that reimburses the mutual fund for the sales commission (usually 4% of money invested in the fund) it pays up front to brokers and others who sell the fund. An investor, even after being in the fund for 20 years, will still be charged this fee to help pay the sales commissions for new money being deposited into the fund by other investors.

   The annual distribution fee is usually 1% of total assets and is an annual charge against earnings (or added to fund losses). The fee is *never* waived and is charged to all investors in the fund.

5. Management Expense Fee: This fee is typically 1% annually and reimburses mutual funds for the expenses incurred in keeping track of investors' funds as well as selecting and pooling investments. It is referred to as the expense ratio by most mutual fund ranking services.

Investment Results Comparison   A 401(k) plan typically offers investments covering four investment categories: money market funds or the guaranteed investment, balanced funds, growth funds, and aggressive growth funds.

A final investment expense is the *opportunity cost* of an investment selection that does not include funds with excellent past performance. Chapter 13 will discuss how to select mutual funds.

Using the Cost Comparison Worksheet
to Analyze Two Plans

The next step is to compare the costs and investment results of two representative plans—one using a packaged approach and the other offering the team approach. In this illustration, the two cost comparisons assume a plan with 50 participants and $500,000 in total assets.

Packaged Plan

Name of financial institution: Insurance Company
Name of administration firm: Insurance Company

Assumptions

Administration Costs

Base Annual Fee:	$1,000
Per Participant Fee:	$35 per participant
Administrative Asset Fee:	1.5% of assets

Investment Management Costs

Money Management Fee:	1% of assets
Up-front Commission:	None
Back-end Fee:	None ongoing, but up to 7% if the plan terminates the mutual fund
Annual Distribution Fee:	None
Investment Results Comparison:	Acceptable

Cost Calculations

	Employer-Paid	Participant-Paid
Administration Costs		
Base Annual Fee	$1,000	None
Per Participant Fee	$1,750	None
Administrative Asset Fee	None	$7,500
Investment Management Costs		
Money Management Fees	None	$5,000
Up-front Commission	None	None
Back-end Fee	N/A	Yes
Annual Distribution Fee	None	None
Investment Results Comparison:	Acceptable	
Total Cost	$2,750	$12,500
Total Annual Plan Cost	$15,250	

Team Approach

Name of financial institution:	No-load Mutual Funds (Janus, Invesco, Twentieth Century, etc.)
Name of administration firm:	Third-party administrator

Assumptions

Administration Costs

Base Annual Fee:	$1,500
Per Participant Fee:	$60 per participant
Administrative Asset Fee:	0.4% of assets

Investment Management Costs

Money Management Fee:	1% of assets
Up-front Commission:	None
Back-end Fee:	None
Annual Distribution Fee:	None
InvestmentResults Comparison:	Acceptable

Cost Calculations

	Employer-Paid	Participant-Paid
Administration Cost		
Base Annual Fee	$1,500	None
Per Participant Fee	$3,000	None
Administrative Asset Fee	$2,000	None
Investment Management Costs		
Money Management Fees	None	$5,000
Up-front Commission	None	None
Back-end Fee	None	None
Annual Distribution Fee	None	None
Investment Results Comparison:	Acceptable	
Total Cost	$6,500	$5,000
Total Annual Plan Cost	**$11,500**	

The package plan produces lower costs to the company sponsoring the 401(k) plan, but the team approach produces lower overall costs. Comparing different plan proposals, then, begins with the Cost Comparison Worksheet. (Appendix A contains a blank Cost Com-

Summary of Examples		
	Package Approach	*Team Approach*
Cost to Employer	$2,750	$6,500
Cost to Participants	$12,500	$5,000
Total Cost	$15,250	$11,500

parison Worksheet that decision-makers can use. This worksheet is more detailed than the worksheet used in the preceding examples, but it follows the example's general outline.)

Cost is but one factor in comparing different plan proposals. All of the advantages and disadvantages of both package plans and the team approach must be considered.

IIIII THE ADVANTAGES OF PACKAGE PLANS

First, package plans can be a cost-effective way to start a plan. Often, if the brokers or insurance agents selling the package plan are conducting all of the employee meetings and performing the other chores required to start the plan, the installation costs are minimal. The financial institution is compensating its salespeople with commissions and is essentially subsidizing the start-up.

For a few early years, then, the low start-up costs and the relatively small account balances can make this approach the cheapest. While the back-end sales charge is a disadvantage, it does grade down and disappear over seven to ten years.

Second, accounting can be performed for individual participants daily instead of for the entire plan quarterly. This makes it easier for participants to move money between investment choices 24 hours a day through telephone transfers. This can appeal tremendously to participants, mainly for psychological reasons. Some will call the day after payday to see if their money has been deposited.

Third, the ability to easily switch investments, access account balances, and have daily valuations can be offered by packaged plans less expensively because of their economies of scale and limited investment selection. All records of the money are in the single database of the financial institution offering the plan.

A small number of regional administration companies can

offer daily valuation services for any group of mutual funds, regardless of fund families. But their administration fees are generally greater than those of a financial institution offering the same service for its own group of funds.

Fourth, if all services related to the plan are performed by one institution instead of by a team of advisors, it is easier to assign accountability for the plan in the event that it falls short of expectations.

Fifth, large financial institutions offering packaged plans have name recognition that often helps to promote the plan. Fidelity, for example, dominates the 401(k) market in New England and is strong in other regions, such as the Silicon Valley area south of San Francisco.

Sixth, a final, albeit dubious, "advantage" of packaged plans is that the cost of the plan can be hopelessly buried in the investment management fee and the earnings; the participants unknowingly pay the cost. For example, an insurance company may administer a 401(k) plan for a very reasonable cost; but the insurance company may then offer only a 5% rate of return on its guaranteed investment contract. The plan could have negotiated a rate of 6.5% by purchasing the same guaranteed contract in the open market. In this example, the difference in return is almost impossible to identify as a cost of administration, and, believe it or not, some plan sponsors would see this as an advantage.

IIIII THE DISADVANTAGES OF PACKAGE PLANS

First, as demonstrated using the Cost Comparison Worksheet, package plans can be more expensive to the entire plan than the team approach, and their costs are sometimes difficult to assess and compare.

Second, the mutual funds offered by most package plans have back-end fees that are assessed if the 401(k) plan ends the relationship with the company providing the mutual fund. This fee reduces the plan sponsor's flexibility to change investments. Many plan sponsors realize—too late—that they are effectively stuck with these package plans because going elsewhere would cost too much; in a plan with $500,000 in assets, a 6% back-end fee equals $30,000!

To mitigate these fees, sometimes the 401(k) plan can select a new investment manager and not allow any new money to be deposited into the original package plan. This starts the clock on reducing the back-end fee over time. Meanwhile, however, the plan is administering both the old and the new investments, which costs more. And most daily valuation systems cannot accommodate any outside investments; thus, both plans must be administered in tandem while waiting for the back-end fees to disappear. Basically, there is no inexpensive escape from back-end fees.

Third, compared to a team approach, a package plan is usually less flexible about investment selection. There can be no investment choices other than those offered by the package plan. Even the stock of the company sponsoring the 401(k) plan will often not be an option because there is no way to incorporate this "rogue" investment into the package plan's huge database.

However, it is this very lack of flexibility that makes these plans a package and therefore more affordable than they would otherwise be.

Fourth, the financial institution administers the package plan from a central geographical location that is often in a different time zone or some distance from the plan sponsor. Effective communication becomes very difficult. (You're at work, they're at lunch, or home in bed—or vice versa.)

Remember, compared to the operation of a conventional pension plan, a 401(k) plan is vastly different: participants can change their investment mix and contribution levels, and they can borrow from their accounts. These factors present a communications and operations challenge wherein the administrator must be prepared to respond to hundreds of thousands of participants from all over the country, each of whom has the right to make unilateral decisions about their accounts.

Many package plans fall short of expectations because they are simply unable to respond to the increased communication levels demanded of 401(k) plans. On paper, these plans may look attractive, assuming all goes well, but the biggest complaint about them is that they make it difficult to solve the problems that inevitably arise.

Fifth, if a package plan is sold through a stockbroker, commissioned financial planner, or insurance agent licensed by the National Association of Securities Dealers (NASD), the plan will almost always have an ongoing sales charge, commission, or marketing fee. This fee is characteristic of 401(k) plans sold through financial service marketing organizations, such as brokerage firms and insurance companies who compensate their salespeople by commissions.

||||| THE NO-LOAD PACKAGED 401(k) PLAN OPTION

The other major distribution channel for packaged 401(k) plans avoids some of the usual disadvantages by adopting more of an "order taking" format. This channel assumes that potential clients already know they need a 401(k) plan or need to improve an existing plan; they do not need to pay someone to sell them. These firms treat 401(k) plans like a commodity that will be sought out by customers. While there is a marketing function, its expense is minimal, and is built into the ongoing cost to the plan.

Unfortunately, almost all package plans aimed at small companies include an ongoing cost for an aggressive marketing function, and this cost clings like a barnacle for the life of the plan. Large pension plans can buy administration with no extra marketing fee from pure no-load mutual fund companies like Fidelity, Vanguard, and T. Rowe Price. Generally, however, smaller companies, with fewer than 200 employees, cannot. For the very small company, a packaged plan without marketing charges simply does not exist. What is "very small"? Today it is defined as fewer than 200 employees. Tomorrow, it could be as few as 50 employees.

||||| THE ADVANTAGES OF THE TEAM APPROACH

First, while the cost of a package plan to the company sponsoring the 401(k) is usually lower than a team approach, the team approach may generate lower total plan costs.

Second, if administration and investment management are performed by different firms, investments can be selected on their own merits, and the best investments can be chosen. With a package plan, the investment returns can be affected by administration costs and subsidies. In the long run, selecting the right investments will contribute the most to the financial success of the plan.

Third, local administration companies usually follow up and attend to details better than package plan administrators. The reason is as follows: an administrator in the same city finds it more compelling to respond to a problem than an administrator 3,000 miles and two time zones away. In a business of details and complexity, there is no substitute for a trip across town to meet and solve problems when they occur. A plan sponsor should not expect a financial institution's local sales representative to straighten out a problem affecting the accounting or tax qualification issues of a plan.

Some major financial institutions that have attempted to administer plans have since retreated from the business because of the problem of long-distance administration. Several major insurance companies have been in and out of the administration business several times over the years. Many investment companies now subcontract with regional administrators and usually find this a more cost-effective way to deliver a 401(k) package. To cover all their bases, Fidelity currently offers what seems like every possible permutation of package plans, including the use of regional administrators as well as their own turnkey, pure Fidelity version.

Fourth, by using individual administrators and investment managers, the plan sponsor has more control over cost allocation. If a plan using a team of advisors shifts more costs to the employer than a package plan would, the plan sponsor can shift some or all of the difference back against the earnings of the plan (that is, to the participants). The plan sponsor is in the driver's seat as to allocating costs and can reallocate them differently from year to year.

Fifth, with a team approach, the plan sponsor can choose from a wide spectrum of investment choices (over 4,000 mutual funds) and can change the investment selections repeatedly at a minimal ($500–$1,000) cost, if funds with no loads and no 12b-1 fees are used. The growing amount of 401(k) money will prompt participant demands for more and different investment choices. Any back-end loads on mutual funds can hinder making a change and embarrass the person who chose that program in the first place.

Back-end fees are rarely, if ever, discussed at any length when programs are being installed. A tremendous advantage, then, of the team approach is that it never requires what is one of the most onerous costs of a 401(k) plan.

ⅡⅢ THE DISADVANTAGES OF THE TEAM APPROACH

First, the regional, "mom and pop" nature of third-party administrators makes quality more difficult to assess. Major financial institutions, by comparison, may be mediocre, but at least they are consistently and identifiably mediocre.

Second, smaller regional administrators may create expensive problems and leave no practical recourse for the plan sponsor. For example, the administrator makes a mistake, and the 401(k) plan discovers that the administrator has no "E and O" (Errors and Omissions) insurance and no assets worth suing for.

Third, smaller administrators may have little depth. They may have two or three knowledgeable professionals one year and be down to a bare-bones staff of clerks the next.

Fourth, to buy their way into the marketplace, some regional firms charge too little and cannot afford the layer of management and experience needed to effectively review completed work. Motorcycling offers a good analogy here. On any given day, anyone can probably make it safely across town on a motorcycle, but only an experienced, trained rider (like a motorcycle police officer) can travel day after day without a serious accident.

An inexpensive 401(k) quote for administration can include the hidden soft-dollar cost of paying another firm to put the plan back together. "Pay us now or pay us later."

Fifth, smaller firms may never be able to offer daily valuation. The investment of time and training to transition from a conventional pension firm (doing quarterly valuations) to one that offers daily valuation is monumental. Most small regional firms will not be able to afford this change in the foreseeable future.

SUMMARY

To administer the 401(k) plan and manage its investments, the plan sponsor can select either a single firm that performs all tasks as a package or team of firms that perform individual functions.

The costs of these two approaches may be difficult to compare because the costs may be allocated differently or be disguised. The starting point in comparing plan proposals is the Cost Comparison Worksheet, which is included in Appendix A.

Package Plans Have Advantages

- The 401(k) plan can be started more inexpensively.
- Participants usually have greater access to their funds because accounting is performed on an individual participant basis.
- It is easier to assign accountability for any problems.

- Daily valuation of accounts is more likely to be offered at a reasonable cost.
- The name recognition of the firm offering the package plan will help promote the 401(k) plan.

Package Plans Have Disadvantages

- Package plans cost the overall 401(k) plan more than does the team approach.
- The presence of substantial back-end fees on many package plans makes it expensive to terminate an investment selection.
- Investment selections are usually limited to choices provided by the firm offering the package plan.
- The plan is administered from a central location some distance from the plan sponsor, which can hinder service.

The Team Approach Has Advantages

- The best investments can be chosen because investment selection is not limited to those offered by a single financial institution.
- Local administrators can service the plan better.
- The plan sponsor can better control the allocation of cost between the employer and the participants.

The Team Approach Has Disadvantages

- The quality of regional administration firms is inconsistent and difficult to assess.
- Small administration firms have limited capital and, thus, may never be able to offer daily valuations.
- Small administration firms have little depth of management and expertise.
- Small administration firms, to buy market share, may not charge enough to adequately service the account, and over time, this can cause serious problems.

Chapter 12

Pulling It All Together: The Decision-Making Matrix

Previous chapters have discussed the characteristics of 401(k) plans and the types of plans offered in the marketplace. This chapter pulls together these two aspects to present a matrix that helps the plan sponsor compare plans on an "apples to apples" basis, considering both the qualitative and quantitative factors of competing plans.

||||| 401(k) PLANS HAVE SIX PRINCIPAL CHARACTERISTICS

The prior chapter demonstrated the use of the Cost Comparison Worksheet, which is a quantitative (hard dollar) measure of 401(k) plans. The plan sponsor should also compare 401(k) plans using six characteristics. Each characteristic presents the plan sponsor with a question of which direction to take; for example, how much of the plan's cost should be paid by the employer and how much by the participants, and should the plan's assets be valued daily or quarterly? Decisions like these must be made by the plan sponsor for each characteristic.

1. Who pays the plan's administrative and investment management cost? And, most important, what's the total cost?

   - Participants
   - Employers
   - Combination of participants and employer

2. How are the plan's assets valued?

- Daily
- Quarterly

3. Who is the plan purchased from?

- An organization with a large sales force that actively sells the plan, thereby incurring an annual marketing fee charged to the plan
- An organization with little or no sales force that sells the plan like a commodity in an order-taking environment, thereby incurring little or no marketing cost to the plan

4. How well does the administrator perform the compliance and testing tasks for the plan?

- Adequately
- Inadequately, so that additional resources (such as attorneys or other pension professionals) are needed to bolster the administrator's work

5. How extensive is the communication between the administrator/investment manager and the plan sponsor and participants?

- Communication with plan sponsor
- Administered from a long distance with contact primarily by phone and local sales representative
- Administered locally with visits by the administration company principals scheduled periodically or as problems arise
- Communication with participants
- Little communication except the quarterly statement of each participant's account
- Quarterly statement, plus periodic meetings with participants

6. From how wide a group of mutual funds should the plan's investments be drawn?

- Unlimited, so that the plan sponsor selects from the more than 4,000 mutual funds available today
- Limited to those offered in a package or by a financial institution

These characteristics or decision points are applied to each type of 401(k) plan.

▌▌▌▌▌ SEVEN TYPES OF 401(k) PROGRAMS

The prior chapter discussed how a plan's administration and investment management can be performed by a single organization (a package approach) or by several organizations (a team approach). The package and team approaches can be further divided into seven categories—and virtually all 401(k) plans offered to small companies today fall into one of these categories.

1. Package plan offered by an insurance company

2. Package plan offered by a brokerage firm

3. Package plan offered by a bank

4. Package plan offered by a mutual fund organization like Fidelity

5. Team approach consisting of a regional third-party administrator and no-load mutual funds with quarterly valuation

6. Team approach consisting of a regional third-party administrator and no-load mutual funds with daily valuation

7. Team approach consisting of a regional third-party administrator and no-load mutual funds with quarterly valuation, plus the option of individual account administration on a daily valuation basis at an extra cost to those choosing this option

The Decision-Making Matrix

These seven types of programs can be compared using the six characteristics in the prior section and the Cost Comparison Worksheet in Appendix A (or a spreadsheet program). To illustrate this, the following example uses a 50-participant 401(k) plan with $500,000 in assets. The Annual Plan Cost was calculated using the Cost Comparison Worksheet. In the following comparison of different plans, the "Annual Plan Cost" is expressed as simply the sum of total cost for both employer and participants combined. Step One, after all, is to determine that a plan is a good value. Step Two will be to determine the varying degrees to which the plan's costs will be split between employer and participants.

1:   Package plan offered by insurance company.

Annual Plan Cost:	$18,000 (admin., commissions, money management). Possible termination charge not included in plan cost.
Asset Valuation:	Daily valuation and 800 number.
Plan Seller/Marketing Cost:	Yes. Included in plan cost.
Compliance and Testing:	Weak.
Communication:	Long-distance administration with little employee communication.
Investment Selection:	Limited selection of mutual funds, and the funds underperformed the top-rated mutual funds by 2% per year, an opportunity cost to plan participants of $10,000 annually (2% times $500,000).

2:   Package plan offered by brokerage firm.

Annual Plan Cost:	$18,000 (admin., commissions, money management). Possible termination charge not included in plan cost.
Asset Valuation:	Daily valuation and 800 number.
Plan Seller/Marketing Cost:	Yes. Included in plan cost.
Compliance and Testing:	Weak.
Communication:	Long-distance administration with little employee communication.
Investment Selection:	Large selection of mutual funds but with 12b-1 commissions. (Brokerage firms generally offer a larger—but still limited—selection compared to insurance companies. Also, overall performance of mutual funds is 1% less per year than top-rated funds—an opportunity cost of $5,000 annually (1% times $500,000).

3: Package plan offered by bank.

Annual Plan Cost:	$10,000 (admin. and money management).
Asset Valuation:	Daily.
Plan Seller/Marketing Cost:	None.
Compliance and Testing:	Handled by banking officials and attorneys. Banks generally have good reputations for compliance.
Communication:	Administration usually done locally, because banks tend to be regional organizations. They offer 401(k) services to all businesses but especially those with whom they have a banking relationship.
Investment Selection:	Investments typically limited to bank's own mutual funds, which notoriously underperform comparable top-performing funds by as much as 3% per year—an opportunity cost of $15,000 annually (3% times $500,000). Funds cannot be followed in the newspaper by participants.

4: Package plan offered by mutual fund organization, such as Fidelity.

Annual Plan Cost:	$12,000 (admin. and money management).
Plan Valuation:	Daily valuation with an 800 number.
Plan Seller/Marketing Cost:	None.
Compliance and Testing:	Handled by sales representatives, with no 5500 form preparation.
Communication:	Long-distance administration, with little employee communication.
Investment Selection:	Selection limited to Fidelity's funds, which underperform top-rated funds by 0.5% per year, an opportunity cost of $2,500. (While Fidelity equity funds are excellent, money market funds may be substantially below the top performers.)

5: Team approach consisting of a large regional third-party administrator and a selection of no-load mutual funds. Valued *quarterly*.

Annual Plan Cost:	$12,000 (admin. and money management).
Asset Valuation:	Quarterly valuation.
Plan Seller/Marketing Cost:	None.
Compliance and Testing:	Handled by administration company principals.
Communication:	Local administration.
Investment Selection:	More than 4,000 mutual funds available as investment choices, thus no opportunity cost due to limited investment selection.

6: Team approach consisting of a large regional third-party administrator and a selection of no-load mutual funds. Valued *daily*.

Annual Plan Cost:	$15,000.
Asset Valuation:	Daily valuation offered locally by regional administrator—not by financial institution supplying investments.
Plan Seller/Marketing Cost:	None.
Compliance and Testing:	Handled by administration company principals.
Communication:	Local administration offers better, easier communication.
Investment Selection:	More than 4,000 mutual funds available as investment choices, thus no opportunity cost due to limited investment selection.

7: Team approach consisting of a large regional third-party administrator and a selection of no-load mutual funds, plus the option of individual account administration.

Annual Plan Cost:	$17,000 (assuming ten of the 50 employees elect individual accounts).
Asset Valuation:	Quarterly valuation for all employee accounts. Daily valuation for those participants with individual account administration.
Plan Seller/Marketing Cost:	None.
Compliance and Testing:	Handled by administration company principals.
Communication:	Local administration offers better, easier communication.
Investment Selection:	More than 4,000 mutual funds available as investment choices. Further investment flexibility (including all individual stocks) for any employees willing to pay for individual account administration at a cost of $500 per year. No opportunity cost due to limited investment selection.

These seven types of 401(k) plans represent what the average plan sponsor faces when reviewing a stack of proposals from would-be vendors. No one plan is ever perfect. There are always compromises to be made. However, the two basic building blocks for making informed decisions are appreciating the wide variance in administration quality and understanding the cost components (some of which are well-hidden) of these plans.

Soft-Dollar Costs

One well-hidden cost component is the soft-dollar cost of selecting certain mutual funds, i.e., the cost of poor performance. In comparing types of 401(k) plans, the plan sponsor must distinguish, as in the foregoing comparisons, between the "hard-dollar" or out-of-pocket costs paid by participants and plan sponsors and the "soft-dollar" or opportunity costs of poor investment performance.

The hard-dollar costs are clearly more important, because the soft-dollar costs of poor performance are so difficult to quantify and predict. However, some pension professionals argue that the soft-dollar costs of poor performance are far and away the greater cost. Each plan sponsor must make his or her own judgement on this; the important thing is to make a conscious decision when analyzing the plans, instead of recognizing these costs only in retrospect after the plan experiences poor performance.

The Personal Connection

In the final analysis, the plan sponsor's choice of vendor will depend to some extent on whether they like the people they will work with. Even analytical people often make decisions based on their emotional feelings, and they pick whatever rationale is needed to support what they feel like doing. Preferably, the plan sponsor will feel like working with some great people who are offering a cost-effective 401(k) plan, one that will make the plan sponsor a hero in the eyes of employees and superiors.

If you decide to pay extra for daily valuation, make sure you really feel a need for it. In the minds of some, daily valuation is like having a once-popular hamster or a gerbil that your kids play with only once a week after the novelty has worn off. In the meantime, your nocturnal rodent is spinning his wheel all night long and you're having to feed it every day. An unofficial source formerly employed by a major mutual fund company claims that only 2% of all employees ever call to get their account balances, and 95% of those calls are to determine the amount of their account balance for borrowing purposes. Future surveys will determine whether this anecdotal comment is accurate.

SUMMARY

Virtually all 401(k) plan proposals to small companies fall into seven categories. When plan sponsors screen proposals for their 401(k) plan, the screen should consist of the six quantitative and qualitative characteristics that all plans have.

401(k) Plan Proposals Have Six Characteristics

- Costs can be paid by employees or employers.

- Assets can be valued daily or quarterly.

- The plan can be bought from an organization with a large marketing force and incur significant annual marketing costs or be bought from an order-taking firm and incur little or no marketing costs.

- The administrator can perform all compliance and testing functions or the plan sponsor can hire other pension professionals to assist the administrator with these tasks.

- The plan's investment selection can include all mutual funds available today or include only a small subset of funds, which may or may not include the top-performing funds.

- The administrator can be local and provide a large amount of personal service to both the plan sponsor and employees or can operate from a central location, which may be some distance from the plan, thus hindering communications and personal involvement.

There Are Seven Types of 401(k) Plans

- Package plans offered by
  - Insurance companies
  - Brokerage firms
  - Banks
  - Mutual fund companies
- Team-approach plans offered by large, third-party administration firms with a wide selection of mutual fund investment selections and distinguished by
  - Daily valuation
  - Quarterly valuation
  - The option of individual investment selection

Chapter 13

Selecting Mutual Funds

Mutual funds are now the dominant money management format used by 401(k) plans, especially smaller companies' plans. Thus the question for the plan sponsor is not, "Do I use mutual funds?" but rather, "Which mutual funds do I offer as investment choices for my plan?"

This chapter discusses:

1. The criteria for selecting mutual funds for the plan

2. Information to help plan sponsors select mutual funds for the plan

3. Information to help plan participants select investments.

IIIII PAST PERFORMANCE AND COST ARE THE KEY CRITERIA

There are two primary criteria for selecting a mutual fund for a 401(k) plan: past performance and cost.

Past Performance

Past performance is no guarantee of future performance, but it is a good guide. According to a study at the Harvard Business School, published in the *Journal of Finance* (July 1993), if a mutual fund outperforms its peers in a certain mutual fund category during a one-year period, it will, with a high degree of probability, continue to outperform its peers during the succeeding eight quarters. (This probability of relative success melts away by the eighth quarter, but by then, the mutual fund choices should be reviewed again anyway.)

The study also concluded that the top performing mutual funds consistently produced the best future performance, and the worst performing funds consistently produced the worst future performance.[1]

The study proves that investment strategies derived from even the most simplistic evaluation of past performance can improve risk-adjusted returns in the future. *Mutual Fund Forecaster* has based its advice to subscribers on this premise for years, and it is now one of the most widely read mutual fund ranking services.

Past performance does mean something, and as discussed later in this chapter, there are readily available sources of performance data that plan sponsors can easily access.

Cost

Chapters 10 and 11, which discussed the fees charged by mutual funds, pointed out that most mutual funds selected by 401(k) plans typically charge an annual fee of only 1% or less. However, many so-called no-load funds have hidden fees, and this point is gaining increased attention in the daily and financial press.

An article entitled, "What's My Load?" in *Forbes* (December 1992) has the subheading, "If your 401(k) plan costs you more than a percentage point a year in overhead and portfolio management fees, you're paying too much."

The article continues:

> . . . oh well, you may say, it's only a percent or so. What's the difference? Over time, a lot. Jones puts $1,000 into an investment from which 1.5% is deducted for costs; Smith puts $1,000 into an identical investment with costs of 0.5%. After 30 years, Smith is 35% better off. . . . if your employer is leaving you in the dark about costs you pick up, complain. And if the costs are high, complain loudly. How much is too much? As noted, *any sales load* at all is probably *too much.*[2]

In the *San Francisco Chronicle* (15 November 1993), an article entitled "Beware of Brokers' No-Load Funds" says,

> Hoping to recapture market share lost to no-load funds that sell directly to investors without a sales commission, the brokerage industry is pushing several types of mutual fund shares that appear to eliminate loads but in reality just shift them around. . . . They [these new funds] are easier to sell than tra-

ditional load funds and the brokers still get an upfront commission, often as much as they get selling A shares (traditional load funds). The commission is paid by the mutual fund company which recoups the fee by jacking up the expenses charged to fund shareholders each year.[3]

These mutual funds are referred to as 12b-1 funds, and they typically have a "back-end" commission that is charged only if money is withdrawn from the fund within a certain number of years. Most mutual funds waive these back-end loads for participants in a 401(k) plan. Otherwise, it would be impossible to allocate the back-end load between the participants withdrawing from the fund and those remaining. Believe it or not though, there are some 401(k) plans out there struggling with this impossible situation. Many brokers selling these funds are quick to point out that the back-end load is waived, but they do not carefully explain that in addition to the back-end fee, there is often an annual fee that is part of the annual expense for investors, and *it has not been waived.*

This annual fee adds 0.5%–1% to the cost of owning these funds. Because the fee is charged annually on both the money invested and the earnings, a participant paying a 1% 12b-1 fee during a 20-year period may have paid a commission equal to 35% of all money invested and earned. This phenomenon is the basis for *Forbes* (December 1992) pointing out that 1% over time can chew up as much as 35% of an account.

Here is yet another simple, elegant way to comprehend the magnitude of these fees. Someone depositing $1,000 per year into the plan and paying 1% of the total account balance as a 12b-1 marketing fee is giving up only $10 in year one. By year ten with accumulations of probably $15,000 in the account, the cost is $150 (1% of $15,000). That $150 amounts to 15% of the $1,000 deposited in year ten. By the twentieth year, the account is now approaching $60,000, including tax-free compounded earnings. The 1% now amounts to $600 or 60% of the $1,000 deposited that year. And we thought that these 8% loads were high!

If a mutual fund has excellent past performance, should the sales commission be ignored? No. According to John Markese, president of the American Association of Individual Investors, quoted in the *San Francisco Chronicle* (24 January 1994) article "Fund Fees Can Bite into Profits,"

> . . . in a typical year, when returns are in the single digits, fees can take a much bigger bite out of mutual fund profits. If you look back, you can say "I'd pay 2 percent to get that 30

percent rate of return." But going forward, the only thing you know for sure is the fee.[4]

In the same article, Joe Sinha, a senior data analyst with Morningstar Mutual Funds, says that when he's choosing a fund, fees are the second thing he considers after performance.

> If the fund has a consistently high five-year record, and higher fees, I would buy it. If Fund A and Fund B are really identical, but one has higher expenses than the other, then the choice would be obvious.[5]

A plan sponsor must pay attention to articles like those cited above because they appear in daily newspapers, not just in the financial trade press, and employees read them right after the comics or the sports page. Every company has its group of self-styled mutual fund experts, and these people influence the other participants' attitudes about investments. A 401(k) plan was installed recently at an automobile dealership where the mechanics had elected to leave the union. The company owner was, in his own words, "dumbfounded by the sophisticated questions asked by these mechanics. Some of these guys appear to know more than I do about funds," he said, "and I thought they just lived from paycheck to paycheck."

As investments are being selected for the plan, the plan sponsor must appreciate employee sophistication; the wrong decisions can become an issue and a potential embarrassment—sooner or later.

▐▐▐▐▐ PLAN SPONSORS HAVE MANY SOURCES OF INVESTMENT ADVICE

In seeking advice about which mutual funds to select for a 401(k) plan, plan sponsors have a wide array of sources, some of which have been discussed in earlier chapters. These sources can be classified, generally, in three ways:

1. Relatively inexpensive financial publications and mutual fund rating services

2. Relatively inexpensive outside firms such as financial planners and pension administrators

3. Relatively expensive outside firms like brokerage firms and insurance companies

Inexpensive Financial Publications and Rating Services

The inexpensive (less than $500 per year) sources of investment advice about mutual funds are publications like *Forbes, Fortune, Money, Kiplinger's,* and *Financial World;* and mutual fund rating services like *Morningstar* and *Mutual Fund Forecaster.* They offer a wealth of information regarding the comparable performance of the more than 4,000 mutual funds available today.

All of these publications and services rank the performance of funds in both up and down markets; and, while the methodology of each ranking approach is different, all are reasonably sophisticated. For example, *Morningstar* uses a risk-adjusted rating system that measures risk as well as return. This service is on floppy disks that are updated monthly or quarterly at the client's option. The user, on a personal computer, can screen electronically almost 4,000 mutual funds to create a list of the top-performing funds that fall within a pre-set risk (price volatility) range. Also, these funds can be ranked in some 30 different mutual fund categories, such as international, growth, and value.

In addition to quantitative data, the *Morningstar* service offers voluminous qualitative information on each fund, such as whether the fund's current manager is the same person who generated those great results or is someone new and untested.

Plan sponsors can load up the *Morningstar* software on their PCs for about $400 per year. The sheer entertainment value of generating color graphs and charts that compare your favorite funds is easily worth the $100 per quarter!

Another rating service is BARRA, a publicly owned company in Berkeley, California, which offers elaborate software that allows users to rank money managers and mutual funds by investment style. After identifying 33 different investment styles, the user can determine the volatility of each style and then determine how different money managers have performed relative to their peers who used the same style. Choice of style, interestingly enough, affects risk more than the selection of individual stocks. BARRA's software costs in the neighborhood of $20,000, which may sound expensive to some plan sponsors. However, some fee-only financial planners have this program or something comparable available as part of the research that they offer.

Mutual Fund Forecaster can provide subscribers with the monthly *Mutual Fund Buyer's Guide* as well as a book, *Stock Market Logic,* that outlines the methodology used to determine the imputed value of a stock. In valuing mutual funds, every holding of the fund passes through the stock market logic screen to determine how the fund as a whole will be likely to perform.

Combining these financial publications and rating services with an informal investment committee of interested participants can be an effective way to select mutual funds in a smaller company.

Inexpensive Outside Firms

Financial planners and pension administrators are the primary sources of relatively inexpensive investment advice.

Most financial planners, like brokers, are licensed by the NASD, which allows them to sell commissioned investment products. However, in many cases, financial planners work for only a fee or an hourly rate as opposed to receiving commissions from mutual funds. Financial planners are also distinguished from brokers because they are often sole proprietors who pay their own rent, phones, and other expenses. Because of this independence, financial planners argue that they represent the client more effectively. For example, they can recommend no-load mutual funds, which a broker cannot do.

Another advantage of using a financial planner who is paid with a fee instead of a sales commission is that the plan sponsor controls both the cost and the quality of the service. The work expected of the financial planner, the work performed, and the fee paid are all closely linked.

A plan sponsor should be careful to use a financial planner designated as a Registered Investment Advisor, because anyone giving investment advice must be registered under the Investment Act of 1940. By doing so, the plan sponsor further spreads out some of the fiduciary responsibility.

Pension plan administrators have varying capacities to offer advice regarding mutual fund choices. Many are Registered Investment Advisors, and all have had the experience of working with hundreds of pension plans. This perspective helps them appreciate the investments that have worked well and those that have fallen short of expectations.

Even if pension administrators do not make specific recommendations, they can steer the plan sponsor toward the right sources of information—in some cases, a list of fee-only financial planners. Usually, this assistance comes at little or no extra cost, because it is a part of the general discussion involving the takeover or installation of the plan.

Expensive Outside Firms

The investment offerings of brokerage firms and insurance companies usually involve sales commissions (and the effect of sales commissions was covered earlier in this chapter). Beyond that disadvantage is the potential risk of the relatively narrow selection of mutual funds that brokerage firms and life insurance companies offer.

Large brokerage firms such as Merrill Lynch, Prudential Bache, Smith Barney, Dean Witter, A. G. Edwards, and even small brokerage firms can provide investment advice about which mutual funds to select for a plan, because of the background and training of their stock brokers and investment advisors.

However, plan sponsors must be aware that the brokers can recommend only those mutual funds that generate commissions. Brokers cannot recommend a no-load fund. Advice from brokers, therefore, is not very objective. In the *Mutual Fund Buyer's Guide* (May 1994), 27 of the 37 mutual funds on a top-rated list of five-star funds were pure no-load funds. A broker could have recommended only the remaining ten, which included sales commissions.[6]

Life insurance companies typically offer groups of mutual funds that they feel will have above-average performance. These may be proprietary pools of money managed by their own employees or be conventional mutual funds drawn from a larger universe. The mutual fund selection offered by life insurance companies is usually smaller than that of brokerage firms, and like the brokerage firms, may not include the top-performing funds. The primary engine that drives the choice of funds is the successful negotiation over fee splitting rather than a careful review of performance.

||||| PARTICIPANTS CAN BE ADVISED ABOUT MUTUAL FUND SELECTION

Plan sponsors may want to help individual participants choose an investment mix; or educate them about risk, return, and basic financial fundamentals.

Here, the plan sponsor is edging down a slippery slope. The average unsophisticated participant generally leans toward the most conservative investment selection. Appendix B offers a sample of what I feel the employee needs to know to make an informed decision about investment mix. To go much beyond this and encourage a participant to take more risk may put the plan sponsor in a risky situation.

For the plan sponsor who wants to provide participants with more information, brokerage firms and financial planners provide two sources of information; and for larger plans, a third option exists.

In marketing their investment management services, brokerage firms emphasize that they will routinely update the participants and conduct meetings to offer investment advice. This is, in theory, a partial justification for the commissions they will be paid. In fact though, there is relatively little follow-up from brokerage firms. Brokers are only human: instead of spending an afternoon driving across town to meet with three or four participants whose contributions the brokers have already been paid for, brokers would, understandably, rather spend the time on the phone trying to sell the next 401(k) plan. Finding another plan with $500,000 in assets will pay them a $20,000 up-front commission on the 12b-1 funds that they hope to sell. In reality, the brokers' ongoing education program becomes a vague promise that rarely comes close to being worth the commissions that are a built-in cost of the plan.

Just as plan sponsors can hire financial planners on a fee basis to advise about which mutual funds to select for the plan, the plan sponsor can hire them on a fee basis to help the participants invest their money. Because of financial planners' fee-based approach, the plan sponsor can better control their work and compensation. In contrast, if a broker is used, the plan sponsor must be able to justify to fellow executives (those depositing $10,000 per year into the plan) why they have "paid" an average of $1,000 per year for the broker's help. (This assumes that the broker's commissions increase annual expense ratios by 1% per year, which, in turn, will reduce total accumulations by approximately $10,000 by the end of ten years.)

401(k) plans with more than $1,000,000 in assets have an additional option: a few mutual fund families (such as American Funds and Dreyfus) will pay their first year's management fee to the brokerage firms that bring them a 401(k) plan with at least $1,000,000 in assets. The brokerage firm can then sell the mutual fund to the 401(k) plan without having to charge a front-end or back-end load; this effectively creates a no-load fund for plan participants, and the broker still gets paid. In some cases, the brokerage firms will even use a portion of their commissions to subsidize the administration costs of the plan. This is the purest example of a win-win situation between broker, plan sponsor, mutual fund, and participant.

In the future, we would expect to see more of this, because mutual funds are so profitable on large pools of money. According to John Bogle, in his book, *Bogle on Mutual Funds*, it costs a fund about 70 basis points (out of their 100 basis point fee) to handle a $3,000 account but only six basis points (out of the 100 basis point fee) to handle a $50,000 account.[7] For 401(k) plans with a large pool of money, there are 94 basis points to spend on subsidizing administration and paying commissions. It's time for some mutual funds to step up to the plate.

||||||||||||||||||||||||||||||||||||||||||||||||||||||||||||||||||||||||||||||
SUMMARY

In the final analysis, plan sponsors who are running successful businesses are probably smarter than most of the people trying to sell them 401(k) investment advice. Plan sponsors must become their company's in-house expert on mutual funds. This educational process is a great opportunity to sharpen analytical skills by witnessing "how the pros do it." Knowledge is power, and it can help develop a high performance 401(k) plan that will be free of the expensive influences of any major financial institution. Plan sponsors owe this much to their employees and to themselves.

Investment Advice Is Needed for Two Basic Functions

- Investment advice helps plan sponsors choose the investments to offer in the plan.
- Investment advice helps participants who have investment-related questions.

Plan Sponsors Should Use Two Primary Criteria in Selecting Mutual Funds

- Past performance is a good indicator of future performance.
- Funds that charge a sales commission, or more than a 1% fee are expensive and difficult to justify to participants.

A Wide Array Of Sources of Information Exists to Help Plan Sponsors Select Mutual Funds

- Financial publications and mutual fund rating services are inexpensive sources.
- Financial planners and pension administrators, working for a fee instead of a sales commission represent a good value, and their cost can be controlled.
- Brokerage firms and insurance companies provide a limited selection of mutual funds, and these funds usually include sales commissions.

Investment Advice Exists for Plan Participants

- Appendix B of this book is a primer about making informed investment decisions.
- Brokerage firms have many experienced people to provide help, but the help entails sizable sales commissions.
- Financial planners, working on a fee basis, are a relatively inexpensive source of help.
- For plans with more than $1,000,000 in assets, some mutual funds that normally have sales commissions are sold to the plan on a no-load basis.

Notes

[1] Hendricks, D., Patel, J., Zeckhauser, R., "Hot Hands in Mutual Funds: Short-Run Persistance of Relative Performance, 1974–1988," *The Journal of Finance,* July 1993, p. 93

[2] Geer, C. T., "What's My Load?" *Forbes,* December 7, 1992, p. 76.

[3] Pender, K., "It's Your Money: Beware of Brokers' No-Load Funds," *San Francisco Chronicle,* 15 November 1993, Business Section, p. B4.

[4] Pender, K., "It's Your Money: Fund Fees Can Bite into Profits," *San Francisco Chronicle,* 24 January 1994, Business Section, p. C1.

[5] *Ibid.*

[6] *Mutual Fund Buyer's Guide.* (Fort Lauderdale, FL: The Institute for Economic Research, May 1994.)

[7] Bogle, J.C., *Bogle on Mutual Funds: New Perspectives for the Intelligent Investor.* (New York: Dell Publishing, 1994), p. 198.

Chapter Fourteen

Using Attorneys and CPAs in a 401(k) Plan

While installing and maintaining a 401(k) plan, a plan sponsor will periodically use an attorney or a certified public accountant. This chapter discusses when the plan sponsor may need attorneys and CPAs and how to select them.

IIIII WHEN TO CALL A LAWYER

When legal help is required, the administration firm is the plan sponsor's early warning system. Most pension administrators are equipped to handle routine plan design and administration, which is why their Errors and Omissions insurance is relatively inexpensive. However, in some situations, the administrator will not want to be liable, and good administrators will know when to ask for help.

Attorneys can be used in two primary areas:

1. Drafting and amending documents
2. Solving problems

Drafting and Amending Documents

Traditional pension plan documents were often drafted by attorneys. Today, the vast majority of plans are so-called "pattern" or "regional prototype" plans that have been drafted by law firms and sold in computer software form to the pension administration industry. So who needs attorneys? When? And why?

401(k) Plan Documents To understand the attorney's role today in drafting and amending the documents involved in a 401(k) plan, the plan sponsor must first understand the necessary legal documents and their purposes.

If there were graffiti artists in the pension industry, they would run around town spraying the words "Documents Rule!" Documents play an extremely important role in the ongoing operation of a plan. Plans must operate in strict accordance with their documents; any inconsistency can lead to the plan's disqualification.

Any qualified retirement plan is created as a legal entity by a combination of documents:

1. The trust agreement

2. The plan document

3. The summary plan description

4. The corporate minutes or a corporate resolution

5. The adoption agreement

6. The determination letter

The trust document establishes that the participants' contributions to the plan are in a legal entity (the retirement trust) separate from the financial affairs and ownership of the plan sponsor. Any financial difficulty of the plan sponsor does not affect the assets of the 401(k) plan.

The plan document is probably the most important document, because it describes every aspect of the plan and its administration, such as eligibility, matching contributions, loans to participants, and the allocation of gains and losses.

Drafting the plan document and periodically updating it to comply with tax law changes is a major responsibility of the plan administrator or the plan sponsor.

A summary plan description, which by law must be passed out to employees, supposedly provides a simple explanation of the most basic provisions of the plan. Unfortunately, summary plan descriptions are no longer that simple, because attorneys, wanting to protect themselves, have turned this document into an almost mirror image of the plan document itself. Summary plan descriptions are now so complicated and intimidating that most employees just give up and, instead, focus on the abbreviated promotional materials provided to help them determine whether to participate in the plan. This promotional material now does the job originally intended for the summary plan description.

The corporate minutes or a corporate resolution is the document through which the corporate owners and directors elect to begin (or change) the plan.

The adoption agreement, signed by the board of directors of the company sponsoring the 401(k) plan, translates a pattern plan into one suitable for a specific company. The pattern plan, which has been pre-approved by the Internal Revenue Service as a prototype, spells out every possible provision. The adoption agreement just zeros in on those provisions required to meet the needs of a specific plan sponsor.

The determination letter is the approval by the Internal Revenue Service of the plan. (After the plan is adopted by the company, it is submitted to the Internal Revenue Service for approval.) The determination letter basically says that the government has sprinkled some holy water over the plan. It is a form of insurance policy in case the government, in an audit, ever says that a specific plan provision was not authorized. To operate, a plan does not need a determination letter, but most administrators take this step to protect themselves and their clients.

Attorneys and Compliance   Attorneys can play an important role in customizing a plan to fit a specific company's 401(k) plan and to assure compliance with government regulations. This can occur when a financial institution is the plan's administrator.

If their plan is being administered by Fidelity or another large financial institution, many plan sponsors believe they are absolved of most of their legal responsibility; the financial institutions have batteries of lawyers to review everything and any mistakes will be their problem. This is a false sense of security. A former client, with 800 employees, called me after a year of being with a major financial institution. This client was pleased with the investment performance, but had no confidence in the compliance area. The distinct impression was that data-entry personnel were handling compliance, rather than seasoned pension administrators who understood the nuances of testing, coverage, and the other issues that can lead to disqualification.

401(k) plans offered by financial institutions rarely receive a determination letter from the IRS for a specific plan. Instead, financial institutions use a pattern determination letter, approved by the IRS, which they use for all of their plan-sponsor clients.

Plan sponsors cannot expect the institution's salespeople to know whether that pattern plan fits a specific company's situation.

When plan sponsors use financial institutions as administrators, it's time to call an attorney. The other alternative is to wait for a problem to arise, pay a huge penalty, and then spend five years in court trying to collect the money from the financial institution that sold the plan that was out of compliance.

Attorneys and Plan Amendments and Restatements   Attorneys may also play a role when documents are amended (as they often are) to reflect a change in the operation of the plan or in the tax law. Most tax law changes that affect pension plans have relatively little impact, and just a few simple amendments signed by the members of the plan sponsor's board of directors can bring a plan into compliance with the new laws.

However, occasionally, the change in the law is so far-reaching that the government demands that the entire plan be restated. And this can complicate things. In the case of the Tax Reform Act of 1986, the deadline for restating pension plans was delayed by four years, because the Treasury Department did not provide final interpretations of the law. In the meantime, three additional tax laws that affected pension plans were passed, and no restated pension plan could be submitted to the IRS for approval. Finally, a deadline was set (December 31, 1994) for restating all pension plans, almost eight years after the 1986 tax law. Meanwhile, many plans have been operating in limbo without specific approval (a determination letter) from the IRS. Needless to say, the pension environment during the past eight years has left many gray areas subject to interpretation. In instances like this, an attorney's opinion may provide an insurance policy to protect the plan.

Solving Problems

The fact that attorneys are not called upon to draft plan documents as often as they were ten years ago doesn't sound the death knell for their participation in the pension industry. There is work for both ERISA (pension law) and litigation attorneys in solving 401(k) plan problems.

Attorneys and More Compliance Issues   Just as attorneys can assist with compliance issues in drafting plan documents, they can assist with compliance issues in the plan's operation. In the world of pension administration, issues may require both a legal decision as well as a practical business decision. For example, if an arithmetic or accounting error of a few dollars on an Average Deferral Percentage Test is never corrected, the plan could technically be disqualified. Is this worth a trip to the IRS for a hearing? Technically, yes. Practically speaking, no. A good attorney knows when to jump through hoops and correct a problem by the book, even if it involves a considerable expense, and when to offer a less expensive, possibly more practical alternative. An experienced attorney might say, "That issue has not been the subject of an audit for as long as I've been in the business." Therefore, the plan sponsor can take the chance that it will never come up in an audit, and if it does, a settlement can be negotiated.

There is no quick reference at the IRS that can produce a definitive answer to most problems. Plan sponsors are on their own until the issue comes up in an audit, and then they can only look back at their decision and hope that it was correct, or at least not too aggressive. An attorney can help the plan sponsor make a more informed decision.

A further consideration involves the luxury of client/attorney privilege. If a plan problem becomes serious, the correspondence between an attorney and the plan sponsor/client is not available to the IRS through depositions or the standard fact-finding, pre-trial process. However, communications between the plan administrator and the plan sponsor *are* available. This confidentiality can prompt plan sponsors to use their attorneys early in the problem-solving process.

Attorneys and Litigation   Ever-growing 401(k) account balances and participant control over them, coupled with expectations about rates of return, will create more potential for legal disputes in the future. (People who can demand and afford good legal help will use it.) As a result, more issues and legal problems will arise.

Jurisdiction   All ERISA-related issues that go to court fall under the federal court system, and many federal judges are reasonably knowledgeable about pension issues. These issues are usually "big ticket" items. Back in the mid-1980s, one attorney for a major law firm in New York City billed over $6,000,000 in fees in one year for work on pension issues, mostly involving mergers and acquisitions.

The United States Department of Labor also has jurisdiction over pension plans, but its staff is so overworked that it rarely involves itself in behalf of employees. I recently called the department to see if it would pursue an issue that could have involved a

$300,000 contribution in behalf of employees. I was told that the department could not look at any issue involving less than $1,000,000. However, this may be changing as the number of Department of Labor audits increases.

Choosing the Right Attorney

Large law firms often relegate smaller clients to younger, less experienced attorneys. This can be a problem in pension situations, because the quality of advice depends so much upon experience rather than upon legal research or academic pension knowledge.

A smaller firm, in contrast, with at least one principal who specializes in pension law, will usually provide more seasoned legal help for the plan sponsor. The plan sponsor's administration company is usually the best reference source for legal help, unless the plan sponsor is planning to sue the administrator.

IIIII CPAs ARE ALSO IN THE PICTURE

Having outlined the need for attorneys, we can now move on to talk about one of the biggest burrs under the saddle of a 401(k) decision-maker: the audit of the form 5500.

This government requirement is a make-work project if there ever was one. In plans handled by administration companies, money must be accounted for or the administrator is liable; so why is a CPA needed? The audit's rationale is that plan sponsors are not required to hire a pension administration company; plan sponsors could self-administer the plan and do everything wrong—to the detriment of participants. Also, plan sponsors who did hire administration companies could collude with them and abuse the rights of plan participants, if not steal money outright. It is possible to see this rationale, but for most plans managed professionally, this requirement is a major irritant.

When Audits Are Required

For all 401(k) plans with over 100 employees eligible for the plan, the form 5500 submitted to the government must be audited by a certified public accountant.

If the number of eligible participants hovers above or below 100 from year to year, the plan can sometimes avoid an audit, even if the participants exceed 100 in a given year. Plan sponsors should make sure their administrators are reading these rules carefully, and they may avoid the audit expense in some years.

Audits are also not required until the plan has operated for at least 12 months. Thus, the audit is generally not required for the partial first year that plans operate. This can cause plan sponsors to be surprised when audits are required for the plan's second year of operation, because in many cases, any discussion about the audit occurred two years earlier and has long since been forgotten.

The Cost of the Audit

For a plan with about 200 participants, the audit will typically cost $3,000 to $8,000 per year. There are several ways to lower audit costs. First and most important, the plan sponsor should use a local, relatively small accounting firm that has at least one CPA who devotes some portion of his or her practice to pension plan audits. The plan sponsor should commit to using that firm over a period of several years to provide continuity and to avoid reinventing the wheel every few years.

Larger national firms must build the cost of layers of management into the audit. There are no economies of scale applicable to performing audits, so, as a general rule, larger firms just wind up charging more money. Larger accounting firms also tend to send out their newest trainees to do these audits, so everyone spends time teaching these folks the pension business; this is an additional soft-dollar cost in using larger firms.

Audit costs can also be lowered by selecting simple investments, such as mutual funds, and avoiding wrap accounts. Wrap accounts, in which individual money managers trade stocks, are a disaster in a 401(k) plan. Each security is counted as a separate investment. By contrast, mutual funds do all the accounting related to the securities they trade, and the 401(k) plan considers the mutual fund a single investment. Wrap accounts are much more cumbersome to audit—and therefore much more expensive.

‖‖‖
SUMMARY

It is always a little annoying when professional help must be added to a business transaction, and that happens when attorneys and accountants are used in the 401(k) plan. However, like other 401(k) vendors, the plan sponsor must understand how to use them effectively, because the price of not using them when necessary can be staggering. Taking advantage of every possible edge is important; a good attorney and CPA can be the plan sponsor's edge.

Attorneys Have an Occasional Role in Drafting Documents and Solving Problems

- The creation of a 401(k) plan requires the following documents:
  - A trust agreement, which establishes the plan as separate from the company sponsoring it
  - A plan document, which describes the operation of the plan
  - A summary plan description, which restates the plan document in simple language
  - The corporate minutes or corporate resolution, which confirms approval by the company to establish the plan
  - The determination letter from the IRS, which approves the plan
  - The adoption agreement, which translates the provisions from a pre-approved, pattern document to fit a specific company's plan.
- Even though most 401(k) plan documents are based on pre-approved prototypes supplied by administrators, attorneys can review and customize these documents to better fit a company's situation and comply with government regulations.
- When problems arise, the plan sponsor is ultimately responsible, so it's imperative that he or she understands when to turn to an attorney for help.

CPAs Have a Role in Any 401(k) Plans with More Than 100 Employees Eligible for the Plan

- The form 5500 annually filed with the government must be audited by a certified public accountant if a 401(k) plan has:

  - At least 100 employees eligible to participate in the plan

  - Operated for more than 12 months.

- The cost of the audit ranges from $3,000 to $8,000 annually.

- Usually, a small accounting firm with CPAs experienced with pension audits provides better and less expensive service.

Chapter 15

Questions
and Answers

The final chapter of this book will acquaint decision-makers with a shopping list of issues that do not apply to all 401(k) plans but that can periodically become important in some plans. This chapter serves as the reader's equivalent of a "questions-from-the-audience" portion of an after-dinner speech.

1. If I have technical questions about 401(k) plans that I want to research myself, where is the best place to get answers?

The *401(k) Answer Book,* published by Panel Publishing, is the most user-friendly and comprehensive resource for information. It delves into the minutia of pension administration, using an extremely clear, question-and-answer format that is well indexed.

Tax Facts, published by National Underwriter Corporation, is also an excellent resource, but it is less specific to 401(k) plans. Also, *CFO Magazine* has had a series of articles over the years that illustrated the comparative costs of different vendors, but these articles were aimed primarily at the larger-plan marketplace. A relatively new magazine, *Plan Sponsor*, is an excellent resource.

2. I have a real small company. Isn't a Simplified Employee Pension a better deal for me? Can't I install a type of simplified 401(k) plan and save all these administration fees?

Yes and No. The simplified 401(k) equivalent is called a SARSEP (Salary Reduction Simplified Employee Pension), which you can offer to your employees, but it still must pass discrimination tests before owners can contribute. Participants cannot borrow from these plans, so contributions tend to be smaller than with 401(k) plans, and passing the test is therefore always a problem. The test itself is significantly different than the conventional 401(k) test and harder to pass. In most cases, the opportunity costs due to smaller possible contributions for owners will far exceed any savings in administration costs. Finally, SARSEP vendors do not offer to do the required testing. You have to do it yourself or hire an administration firm to make sure it is done correctly. If anyone selling you a SARSEP says the tests are not a problem because "these plans are not being audited," just show them the door. Major financial institutions selling SARSEP have insulated themselves thoroughly from any of the testing obligations, so don't plan to collect from that bank, brokerage firm, or mutual fund if your plan fails the tests and is disqualified. A small company that saves about $1,000 per year in administration fees by going the SARSEP route will undoubtedly be proven to be penny wise and pound foolish— especially if the investment products in the SARSEP included the cost of sales commissions.

3. What happens in a partnership or an S corporation with a 401(k) plan? Doesn't the calculation of incomes become complicated as the corporation deposits money into the plan?

Yes. A partnership's contribution into the employer discretionary accounts of all employees, including those of the partners, will trigger some very difficult year-end calculations. The corporation's contribution for one partner will affect another partner's gross taxable income in proportion to the second partner's ownership percentage of the firm. The second partner's contribution amount will now be affected by his or her updated income calculation, and so on. Moving into the contribution calculation in a crab-like fashion is the way the job is effectively done, but in fact, it can be accomplished with a simultaneous equation. Many partnerships offering 401(k) plans with employer discretionary contributions get confused and annoyed at the end of every year when the time comes to calculate incomes and contributions. Everyone involved needs to accept the fact that this will never be a simple exercise and that to project these final numbers requires careful teamwork between the pension administrators and the partnership's well-informed, in-house contact person.

4. What are these so-called "non-qualified 401(k) plans"? My insurance broker is encouraging me to consider a non-qualified deferred compensation plan that sounds a lot like a 401(k) but with no testing.

Non-qualified plans are retirement plans that receive no special tax breaks. Because they discriminate totally in favor of owners or highly compensated employees, they *do not qualify* for special tax treatment, and that explains the term "non-qualified." They can be very useful, however, because an executive can take advantage of a corporation's lower tax bracket to build up assets on a tax-advantaged basis. A non-qualified plan with the right choice of investments can also provide some tax shelter on the earnings in the plan. Most non-qualified plans are funded with life insurance contracts, because insurance products offer the advantage of tax-deferred compounding of earnings. So-called "variable life" policies even offer the option of popular mutual funds as investments within the tax-deferred framework of the insurance contract.

If the plan is designed so as to name the plan sponsor as the beneficiary of any life insurance proceeds, the corporation then receives a tax-free windfall of the death benefit upon the death of the executive. While a corporation has an unlimited lifespan, its executives are all going to die sooner or later, even if long after retirement. Eventually, the corporation will receive the death benefits under very favorable tax circumstances, and this explains why many larger corporations offer these programs to their executives. An analysis will show that if a few executives die before life expectancy, the entire plan for all executives may not cost much at all. This is the financial community's closest equivalent to a perpetual motion machine!

The basis of any non-qualified plan is an employment contract between the executive and the employer. To the extent that the company agrees to pay a retirement benefit in return for a reduced current wage, the employee becomes a general creditor of the employer.

These plans can be excellent, but they generally come into play only after the opportunities of a conventional 401(k), with greater and more predictable tax benefits, have been exhausted. For company owners who have substantial incomes and net worths, the non-qualified plan is arguably better than a 401(k)— assuming that current estate and income tax laws don't change significantly.

5. What about 401(k)s and ESOPs (Employee Stock Ownership Plans)? Can the two types of qualified plans be combined in any way?

Yes. A 401(k) plan that offers stock in the plan sponsor's company as one of the 401(k) investment choices is referred to as a "KSOP." With some or all of a 401(k) contribution, the participant can purchase stock in his or her own company with pre-tax dollars.

Also, if the company offers a matching contribution or an employer discretionary contribution into the plan, these contributions can be in the form of company stock. A contribution of treasury stock triggers a tax deduction for the corporation without requiring the expenditure of any cash. Of course, this creates a little dilution for existing stockholders, but those venture capitalists probably weren't suffering anyway. Otherwise, the stock can be purchased from existing shareholders using funds that have been contributed to the plan. In a small, thinly traded public company, this steady purchasing activity can actually help the stock's performance.

6. What about Section 125 Cafeteria or Flexible Spending Plans? Since these are often sold along with 401(k) plans, what is the connection?

A Section 125, or Flexible Spending Plan allows employees to pay for three categories of expenses with pre-tax (tax-deductible) dollars. The three categories are:

1. The employee's portion of any health insurance premiums

2. Childrens' daycare expenses up to $5,000 per year

3. Any other uninsured health-related expenses

Employees elect to have pre-tax payroll deductions contributed into a fund, and these dollars are then tapped to reimburse the employee for any incurred expenses in the categories outlined above. The resulting tax savings create an immediate increase in spendable income for employees. To the extent that employees then deposit money into a 401(k), the net effect of the two plans operating simultaneously can set the stage for a 401(k) contribution that does not reduce spendable income or "take-home" pay. It is relatively easy and cost-effective to install a Section 125 during the same employee meetings that introduce the 401(k). The combination of both plans generally enhances participation in the 401(k).

An employee's Section 125 contribution reduces income for *all* tax calculations, so the employer saves what would have been the cost of social security and workers compensation premiums. For some companies, this can mean a savings equal to as much as 10%–15% of whatever the employee deposits. These employer tax savings can often add up to more than the ongoing annual administration of both the Section 125 and the 401(k) plan combined.

7. Section 404(c) offers the option of limited liability to plan sponsors if they offer a selection of investments and frequent reporting to employees. Formally complying with the law, however, looks like a lot of trouble and some extra expense. Is it worth it, and how much is really accomplished beyond just taking a commonsense approach to the operation of a 401(k)?

Because Section 404(c) has only recently taken effect (beginning in 1994), no one really knows. Many aspects of this regulation are subject to interpretation. For example, reporting must be done at least quarterly "or as often as necessary based on the volatility of the investment." What could that possibly mean? *Any* investment short of money market funds was volatile in 1987. The plan must designate a fiduciary and announce formally to employees that the plan fiduciaries may be relieved of liability for any loss resulting from the participant's investment direction.

The participant can legally refuse to direct the investments. If this is the case, the fiduciary may not choose a default investment but must follow the prudence and diversification requirements of Title I of ERISA. The board of directors must formally adopt the provisions of 404(c) with special corporate minutes, and participants must be formally notified that they are now participating in a plan that complies with 404(c). They have the legal right to demand a report of all expenses of the plan and its investments each quarter.

In short, compliance with 404(c) is a great deal more than just calling your broker and asking for a few more investment choices. Yet, in the name of "404(c) compliance," that is often all that happens. A rude shock awaits those who think they have officially limited their liability just by moving to daily valuation and adding a few more investment choices. In the final analysis, you always have some liability and an obligation to do the right thing in behalf of employees regardless of whether you have spent additional time and money to comply with 404(c).

8. What happens to 401(k) account balances when participants die?

A surviving spouse can roll the money over into an IRA and avoid paying a tax. If there is no surviving spouse, the funds are taxed as regular income as they are paid out to beneficiaries, *but they are also subject to estate taxes as well*. For a widowed executive whose total estate is approaching $1,000,000 (including any retirement plan account balances), the effective marginal state and federal income and estate taxes on a distribution to heirs can total as much as 85%! Unfortunately, this often comes as a surprise to those who have done little or no estate planning.

9. What is the story with IRA accounts once a company establishes a 401(k)? Can they be of any further use at all?

IRA accounts continue to have many uses. First of all, a terminating employee can roll money over into a roll over IRA. A roll over IRA is one whose only contributions have come as a result of a participant's termination from a qualified retirement plan. By comparison, a "contributory IRA" is one whose contributions have come as a result of an individual's annual election to make a pre-tax IRA contribution. If a roll over IRA is never "contaminated" by an annual contribution (in other words, it consists purely of money that was at one time in a pension plan), then this roll over IRA can be rolled on into a new 401(k) plan at the next job or any subsequent job that the participant might have.

A participant should be advised that it is not wise to roll money forward into another 401(k), because by leaving it in an IRA account they will have complete investment flexibility with the funds. They can choose any investment mix from among 4,000 mutual funds. Once they have rolled into the next 401(k), they are stuck with whatever the new plan offers for investments. They may even be stuck paying commissions or fees. Once the money is rolled, they lose the ability to take it back out and establish their own IRA again unless they terminate employment. The one advantage to rolling money forward into the next 401(k) plan is the advantage of being able to borrow from the account. For some younger employees, rolling a prior account balance forward may increase the total amount they can borrow and therefore allow them to meet their interim financial goals sooner. The best advice is to tell participants not to roll old funds into a new 401(k) until they specifically need the money for a loan. Discount brokerage firms or large no-load mutual fund families represent the best IRA opportunities for roll over IRAs.

Contributory IRAs are still possible even after a 401(k) has been installed. Single participants with incomes below $25,000 and married participants with incomes below $40,000 can still contribute to IRAs and receive a full tax deduction. Partial deductions are still possible if incomes are slightly higher. Anybody can contribute to an IRA with after-tax dollars and receive the value of tax-deferred IRA earnings regardless of whether they have maxed out on their 401(k) contributions. An after-tax contribution may not sound that enticing until we recall that the major advantage of any tax-deferred opportunity is not the deductibility of the contribution; but rather, it is the tax-deferred compounding of interest. In a small-company environment, it may make sense to offer to pay the taxes on a $2,000 IRA contribution for a participant rather than having a highly compensated employee cluttering up the 401(k) test when their total 401(k) contribution represents a high percentage of income. In a test that is failing, redirecting a portion of the managers' contributions into IRA accounts (and paying their taxes) might make economic sense for a company owner.

IRA accounts, then, are still useful. They are the vehicles through which 401(k) plans can offer "portability" or the participant's ability to carry 401(k) account balances from job to job. They also offer the vehicle through which tax benefits on 401(k) earnings can be preserved long after the participant has terminated employment.

Conclusion

Many other questions arise pertaining to 401(k) plans. However, the purpose of this book has been to focus on the pivotal decision-making points that I feel contribute the most toward the success of a plan. A "Five Star" 401(k) can mean millions of extra dollars, over time, to you and your fellow employees. Self-serving advice from

401(k) vendors can easily stand in the way of a popular, smooth-running plan that would otherwise have met your expectations. Armed with this book, you will no longer be held hostage to a lack of objective information. Your future 401(k) decision making will be the product of balanced, reasoned thinking.

In the meantime, feel free to anoint yourself as your company's own "MR or MS 401(k)." I am confident that you will make the most of your exalted status and enjoy the daily accolades from your appreciative fellow employees. A wealthy gentleman depicted in a *New Yorker* cartoon once said, "I owe my success to some advice I got from my father. He said, 'Son, here's a million bucks. Don't lose it.'" In the same spirit, you and your employees have been given the opportunity to save a million dollars and much more. Don't let bad decisions cost you any portion of that opportunity.

APPENDIXES

Cost Comparison Worksheet

Name of financial institution: _____

Name of administration firm: _____

Assumptions

Administration Costs

    Base Annual Fee: _____

    Per Participant Fee: _____

    Administrative Asset Fee: _____

Investment Management Costs

    Money Management Fee: _____

    Up-front Commission: _____

    Back-end Fee: _____

    Annual Distribution Fee: _____

Investment Results Comparison: _____

Cost Calculations	*Employer-Paid*	*Participant-Paid*
Administration Cost		
Base Annual Fee	_____	
Per Participant Fee	_____	
Administrative Asset Fee	_____	
Investment Management Costs		
Money Management Fees	_____	_____
Up-front Commission	_____	_____
Back-end Fee	_____	_____
Annual Distribution Fee	_____	_____
Investment Results Comparison:	_____	_____
Total Cost	_____	_____
Total Annual Plan Cost	_____	_____

Definitions

Administration Cost

1. **Base Annual Fee:** This fee is usually a fixed dollar amount.
2. **Per Participant Fee:** This fee is based on the number of employees who contribute to the plan and/or on the number of *eligible* participants, regardless of whether they contribute to the plan.
3. **Administrative Asset Fee** (or fee for special services): This fee, if charged, is typically 0.2% to 1% of assets.

Investment Management Fees

1. **Money Management Fee:** This fee is charged against the plan's earnings (or against principal in years when an investment loses money).
2. **Up-front Commission:** Sales commissions are subtracted from investments in a mutual fund, but these are almost unheard of in today's 401(k) plans.
3. **"Back-end" 12b-1 Fee:** These fees are charged if money is removed from the mutual fund. If fund redemptions exceed deposits, a fee of as much as 7% is applied against the money withdrawn; typically, the fee reduces each year and reaches zero after seven to ten years.

   This fee is almost impossible to administer; it is usually waived for individual participants in 401(k) plans. However, 12b-1 fees are retained for the overall plan; if the plan cancels a mutual fund, the back-end fees are charged against the money withdrawn.

   Instead of the mutual fund back-end 12b-1 fee, the life insurance industry uses an "annuity wrap fee." By putting mutual funds inside an annuity (a life insurance product), the 401(k) plan can be sold by life insurance agents who might otherwise lack a securities license.

4. **Annual Distribution Fee:** This is a second form of 12b-1 fee that reimburses the mutual fund for the sales commission (usually 4% of money invested in the fund) it pays up front to brokers and others who sell the fund. An investor, even after being in the fund for 20 years, will still be charged this fee to help pay the sales commissions for new money being deposited into the fund by other investors.

The annual distribution fee is usually 1% annually and is charged against earnings (or added to fund losses). The fee is *never* waived and is charged to all investors in the fund.

5. **Management Expense Fee:** This fee is typically about 1% annually and reimburses mutual funds for the expenses incurred in keeping track of investors' funds as well as selecting and pooling investments. It is referred to as the expense ratio by most mutual fund ranking services.

Investment Results Comparison or Opportunity Cost Calculation

A typical 401(k) plan might offer investments covering six investment categories: money market funds or the guaranteed investment, an index fund, a balanced fund, a growth fund, an aggressive growth fund, and an international fund. A final investment expense, then, is the *opportunity cost* of an investment selection that does not include funds with excellent past performance.

Guaranteed Investments To arrive at an estimated numerical cost for the investment results comparison, begin with a comparison of the historical rates of return on the guaranteed accounts. These are reasonably "hard" numbers and should be approximately the same for all institutions. In cases where the rate of return is lower than competitors, the institution is paying a lower return to subsidize the cost of the administration. A difference in performance on this investment selection is just as costly and as predictable as a per-participant charge or a percentage charge for money management. However, it is routinely ignored in cost comparisons when it may be one of the single largest cost components.

Index Funds Index funds are important to compare with regard to management costs, because an index fund, by definition, is only buying a cross section of stocks. There is no cost of actively managing the account, and any variance of management fees between funds will inhibit performance and generate a hidden administrative cost for participants. For example, a Vanguard S&P 500 index fund charges an annual fee of 0.19% of assets per year. Fidelity's S&P 500 index fund charges 0.45% per year—a difference of 0.26%. A 401(k) whose participants are contributing $100,000 per year into

Fidelity's index fund option will have been charged an extra $25,000 in ten years and about $200,000 in twenty years compared to the result they would have achieved with Vanguard. Theoretically, all index funds of the same type generate the same rate of return, so management fees become the only variable.

Equity Funds   With equity fund comparisons, the opportunity cost is more difficult to quantify, but a general history of poorly-performing funds when compared against a selection of MORNINGSTAR "Five-Star" or FORBES "A-Rated" funds would definitely represent an opportunity cost.

To calculate an approximate dollar figure for this section of the cost comparison, assume that about one third of the funds are in the guaranteed accounts and that the remainder is spread evenly across the remaining funds. With hypothetical account balance figures for each year, calculate the average cost in dollars based upon the percentage return differences over the past five years.

Admittedly, this final portion of the Cost Calculation Worksheet becomes an extremely inexact science, but it makes at least an attempt to factor some performance criteria into the cost comparison between several plans.

What Employees Need to Know About Investing

This appendix presents a short but comprehensive treatise on what employees need to know about choosing investments. Plan sponsors could copy this appendix verbatim, distribute it to their employees, and feel comfortable that the employees have the basic information needed to begin determining their 401(k) investment mix.

This material also provides a review for decision-makers and plan sponsors who have been too busy running their companies in recent years to dwell on the fundamentals of investing.

A further step might be to round up some books on investing and maintain a company library. In addition, if you subscribe to any of the mutual fund rating services, such as *Mutual Fund Forecaster* or *Morningstar*, make those publications available to employees who express an interest. Browsing through the updated rankings each month can be an edifying experience, and beyond just the rankings, these publications always have several pages of narrative comments on the economy and financial markets in general.

"You can lead a horse to water, but you can't make him drink." This axiom applies to your obligation to dispense investment information to employees. If you have offered some version of this appendix and have made other publications available, your conscience should be clear—and your liability will be about as limited as it can be.

How to Choose Your Investment Mix

by Stephen J. Butler
Pension Dynamics Corporation

What Are Your Choices When It Comes to Investments?

Like the basic food groups, there are categories of investments that include savings accounts, bonds, stocks, real estate, and hard assets like gold. Historically, looking back to the turn of the century, stocks have performed the best of all of these groups. The average stock has generated returns about six percent higher per year than the average rate of return on savings accounts or 30-day United States treasury notes.

Where Can I Find an Investment Guru I Can Afford?

If investments in stock appear to represent one of the better approaches to long-term success in retirement planning, the average investor needs access to a means of investing that taps into the know-how of seasoned professional investors—investment managers with proven track records of success in the stock markets. To be practical and cost-effective, the services of these advisors need to be available with ease and minimal cost.

Mutual funds provide the opportunity to invest in a professionally managed investment pool that purchases stocks in hundreds of different companies across the country. As you contribute money into this pool by buying shares in your mutual fund, you effectively buy a percentage of all stocks owned by this pool. Every single business day, the value of the entire pool is calculated based on the price of each share owned by the pool on that day. The total may be hundreds of millions of dollars. You actually own what would be a small percentage of all those stocks and the value of your investment would go up or down on a daily basis as the stocks owned by the pool change in value. If you want to cash in your account, the mutual fund company sells enough of the stock it owns to generate the cash needed for a disbursement to you on that day.

The advantage of a mutual fund is that it offers the novice or small investor some access to the best investment managers in the world. It also offers diversification so that even small amounts of money are spread out over hundreds of different stocks. Finally, there is the protection afforded by the fact that the underlying stocks purchased by the fund secure the investment. The investor's account is always worth its proportionate share of all the stocks owned by the fund.

How Do Stock Market Mutual Funds Compare, Return-Wise?

If you had invested $1,000 in an average-performing stock mutual fund 20 years ago, that $1,000 would have grown to $8,500 today, according to Lipper Analytical Services, a mutual fund tracking service. And that was just the average fund. Some top-ranking funds could have turned your $1,000 into almost $40,000 in the same period. By comparison, the same $1,000 invested in U.S. Government treasury bills would have grown to $4,400 in the same 20 years. $1,000 in a savings account at 5% per year would have grown to $2,600.

Each additional percentage point of interest earned, over time, can translate into millions of extra dollars in the future. The following matrix illustrates even further the extent to which this is true:

$10,000 per Year Investment

Interest Rate	10 Years	20 Years	30 Years	40 Years
2.5%	$112,034	$255,447	$439,027	$674,026
5.0%	$125,779	$330,660	$664,388	$1,207,998
7.5%	$141,471	$433,047	$1,033,994	$2,272,565
10.0%	$159,374	$572,750	$1,644,940	$4,425,926

As previously mentioned, the stock market, historically, has averaged a 6% per year better rate of return than money market funds (or U.S. government short-term Treasuries). If this is the case, why would anyone with at least 20 years until retirement choose to relegate themselves to a money market fund at 5% versus the stock market at, say, 10%? The matrix above shows that in just 20 years, the difference between the money market account ($330,659) and the stock market ($572,749) would be $242,090. This is an expensive price to pay for being too conservative. In 30 years, the opportunity cost (or cost of being conservative) rises to $610,946. This assumes contribution levels of $10,000 per year. At $1,000 per year, the difference is still over $60,000!

That's an Amazing Difference. How Do the Professional Managers Do It?

Managers review specific industries and monitor prices of the stocks in those industries. They tap vast resources of data not practically available to the small investor. They monitor, for instance, the buying and selling activity of corporate officers (known as inside sales), which is public information by law. They also monitor the macroeconomic scene to determine major economic swings and to assess how these will affect stock values. From time to time, they may pull money out of the stock market and leave it parked in cash until less volatile buying opportunities arise.

A major factor in overall success is diversification. While one stock may prove to be a loser, the gains from others can more than offset the loss. An individual investor would find it impossible to achieve the diversification offered by participation in a mutual fund.

What Types of Mutual Funds Can We Choose From?

The most basic division of fund types is between stock funds and bond funds. When you buy stock in a company, you actually own a portion of the company and your investment goes up and down as the company grows or contracts or becomes more or less profitable. Bonds, on the other hand, are loans to companies. A bond investment is a loan to a company that pays a specific rate of interest and that has a beginning and an ending time period. When a bond "matures," the bond-holder gets his or her original money back and, of course, they get to keep the interest earned during the years the loan or bond was in force. Bonds are safer than stocks. If a company goes "down the tubes" the bond holders get whatever money or assets are available first, and the stockholders get whatever is left—if anything.

Which Categories of Funds Have Which Types of Investments?

The major categories of funds are outlined as follows, starting with the riskiest:

Aggressive growth funds buy stock in higher risk companies that offer potential for fast growth, but the values of these companies can be highly volatile and can go down as easily as they can go up.

Growth funds invest in established companies that have remaining potential for further steady growth. They may be introducing new products or opening up world markets. The downside risk is minimal, but the upside potential is great because of these new developments. We're investing in older dogs who are continually learning new tricks. The GAP stores, for instance, had their stock rise by almost 50% in 1991 alone, yet this company has been around for over twenty years.

Growth and income funds invest in stocks of companies that tend to pay high dividends to stockholders. Dividends paid on stocks are like the interest paid on bonds. It is the payment to the stockholder for having an ownership interest in the company. Some companies traditionally pay high dividends because there is little potential for growth. Utility companies like PG&E, for instance, pay high dividends, and owning their stock is almost like owning a bond that pays interest. A mutual fund looking for growth and income will focus first on investments that generate regular dividend income. Then, among those investments, they will look for the ones that demonstrate the most potential for some growth in value as well.

Balanced funds lean further toward income and away from growth. In many cases, half of the money will be invested in bonds, which will ensure a steady flow of interest income on at least half of the money. The other half invested in stocks will generate dividend income and possibly some growth in value over time.

Bond funds invest only in bonds. A bond fund typically pays a higher rate than a money market fund, because the bonds are bought with longer maturities, perhaps an average of ten years. This means that every bond purchase creates, in effect, a ten-year loan.

Because loans of this duration involve more risk, interest rates paid are higher than what the U.S. government pays on the 30- and 60-day notes (bonds) that it sells to money market funds. The so-called "High Yield" Bond Funds buy "junk bonds." These bonds are very high risk bonds or loans to companies that were considered to be really risky from the beginning. People bought junk bonds, however, because these bonds paid interest rates of between 14% and 18% per year. At those rates, the theory went, it didn't matter if a few companies went belly-up. The high interest on the ones that survive would more than compensate.

The Difference Between Bond Funds and Money Market Funds

Money market funds buy very short term loans (30 to 60 days), which involve virtually no risk. The rate paid on a money market is virtually just about the rate of inflation, because lenders are taking no risk and only want to receive enough interest to keep them in line with their loss of money due to inflation.

Bond funds invest longer term. It is possible for a portfolio of bonds to go down in value even though there are no defaults and all interest is paid currently. This happens when interest rates in the open market have risen and the original bonds owned by the fund are paying at their original rate. The value of those bonds in the open market would go down because they now compete with new bonds that pay a higher rate. By the same mechanism, bond mutual funds can rise in value if interest rates on the open market happen to fall. When market rates fall, those original bonds paying a higher rate are suddenly worth more money if we wanted to sell them. Bond mutual funds, like stock funds, are totally valued every business day based on the market value that day of every single bond in the fund.

So How Do These Different Funds Help Me Reach My Goals?

To determine which fund or combination of funds makes the best sense for you, you need to ask the question that forms the cornerstone of any investment program:

When do I plan to need this money?

If you have a long time before the need occurs, you can lean toward stocks and benefit from what will probably be a higher rate of return. If you are saving for a shorter-term goal, then balanced funds or even bonds and money markets can make better sense.

If you are using your 401(k) plan to save for a down payment on a home in the near future, the money market is the best vehicle for your savings. The money will be there for certain when you need it, and the difference in return over just a few short years will not mean that much in actual dollars to be worth the risk of a possible loss.

If you are saving a portion of your 401(k) for a child's college education ten years from now, you might be better served by a balanced fund or a growth and income fund. Ten years is plenty of time for the market to go through a few cycles, so you will probably experience some dramatic gains in at least some of the years. If history repeats itself, you will generate a larger fund in ten years than would have been the case in a money market fund.

If you are saving a portion of your money for retirement itself many years from now, you will be best served by pure growth funds and maybe an aggressive growth fund for a portion of the money. Aggressive growth funds can generate heart palpitations in some markets, but if your fund drops precipitously, you need to always remember why you bought it in the first place and try to resist the urge to sell it. The fund that drops 30% today may earn back 100% over the next two years. It's the old question of whether you want to eat well or sleep well. Try to take as much risk as you feel comfortable with, and never let yourself suffer any regret for the years when, in retrospect, you realize that you should have been more aggressive.

Marginal Tax Rates and the 401(k) Money Machine

The first step toward a full appreciation of your 401(k) opportunity is to gain an understanding of how the government taxes your income. Generally speaking, you don't pay much in taxes on the first half of your income. Instead, the government chooses to really "sock it to you" on the last half of your income. It's the old practice of taxing at an ever-increasing percentage as your income goes up.

Remember the last time you received what was supposed to be a $100 raise per paycheck? You probably noticed that your new take-home pay increased by only about $65. The reason the increase was small compared to your gross wage increase was because that raise was the last $100 of your income and was taxed at the highest rate you pay.

The schedule on the next page will help you calculate the tax rate on each additional amount of money you receive in income. These tax percentages are known as your *marginal tax rates* because they illustrate the rate you pay at the outer limit of your income.

Approximate "marginal" income tax percentages

*(Percent tax on the last $1000 of income;
includes both Federal and California state taxes)*

Single Persons Taxable Income			Tax %	Married Persons* Taxable Income			Tax %
0	to	4,666	16.0	0	to	9,332	16.0
4,667	to	11,059	17.0	9,333	to	22,118	17.0
11,060	to	17,453	19.0	22,119	to	34,906	19.0
17,454	to	24,228	34.0	34,907	to	48,456	34.0
24,229	to	30,620	36.0	48,457	to	61,240	36.0
30,621	to	106,190	40.3	61,241	to	212,380	45.3
106,191	to	212,380	46.0	212,381	to	424,760	49.6
212,381	and over		50.6	424,761	and over		50.6

If your spouse is also working, use your combined incomes to estimate your marginal income tax brackets.

Remember, for each exemption you claim, subtract $2,350 from your taxable income.

IIIII THE 401(k) MONEY MACHINE

(Assumes compound interest @ 8%)

Table A assumes the following adjusted gross incomes

If single: 11,060 to 17,453; If married: 22,119 to 34,906

If you deposit this much per mo.	It will cost approx. this much take-home pay	This is what you will have in					
		3 years	5 years	10 years	20 years	30 years	40 years
$ 20	$ 16	$ 811	$ 1,469	$ 3,659	$ 11,780	$ 29,807	$ 69,820
50	40	2,026	3,673	9,147	29,451	74,518	174,550
75	60	3,039	5,510	13,720	44,176	111,777	261,825
100	80	4,053	7,347	18,294	58,902	149,036	349,100
200	160	8,107	14,695	36,589	117,804	298,072	698,201
400	320	16,214	29,390	73,178	235,608	596,144	1,396,402
600	480	24,321	44,085	109,767	353,412	894,216	2,094,603

Table B assumes the following adjusted gross incomes

If single: 17,453 or more; If married: 34,906 or more

If you deposit this much per mo.	It will cost approx. this much take-home pay	This is what you will have in					
		3 years	5 years	10 years	20 years	30 years	40 years
$ 20	$ 13	$ 811	$ 1,469	$ 3,659	$ 11,780	$ 29,807	$ 69,820
50	33	2,026	3,673	9,147	29,451	74,518	174,550
75	49	3,039	5,510	13,720	44,176	111,777	261,825
100	65	4,053	7,347	18,294	58,902	149,036	349,100
200	130	8,107	14,695	36,589	117,804	298,072	698,201
400	260	16,214	29,390	73,178	235,608	596,144	1,396,402
600	390	24,321	44,085	109,767	353,412	894,216	2,094,603

Index

About the Author
Stephen J. Butler

Mr. Butler is currently the President and Co-founder of Pension Dynamics Corporation, a regional pension consulting and administration firm in the San Francisco Bay Area. He has worked in the pension and employee benefits area since the early 1970s, and has been credited with some of the earlier Employee Stock Ownership Plans and 401(k) plans installed in Northern California.

A graduate of Harvard College (B.A. class of '66) Mr. Butler then attended the University of California Graduate School of Business Administration at Berkeley. Prior to receiving a degree, he left to serve on active duty for the United States Army as an officer in the Medical Services Corps during the Vietnam Era, and later returned to civilian life to work for the Provident Mutual Life Insurance Company. In 1974, he co-founded an employee benefits company, Porter, Butler, Weber.

In 1980, he co-founded Pension Dynamics Corporation, which, since 1984, has specialized in designing and installing 401(k) plans. Operating as a so-called "third-party administrator," Mr. Butler's company has remained independent of major financial institutions such as banks, insurance companies, and stock brokerage firms. This independence has set the stage for offering pure no-load funds as investment choices for plans which, in turn, has contributed to the popularity of such plans.

Within the pension industry, where he is a popular speaker, Steve Butler is best known as a leading advocate of 401(k) plans. In case anyone misses the point, his California automobile license plate reads "MR 401K."

The author's family includes his wife, Frances, who is a psychiatric social worker (MSW and Licensed Family Therapist) working for Battered Women's Alternatives. She also maintains a private

185

practice couseling victims of family violence. Their children include a daughter, Elsa Butler, who is a freshman at Colorado College; and a son, Mason, who attends Acalanes High School in Lafayette, California.

Mr. Butler's other interests include skiing, tennis, golf, sailing, motorcycling, furniture making, and playing bass violin in a jazz trio.

He can be reached at the following address and phone number:
Pension Dynamics Corporation
985 Moraga Road #210
Lafayette, CA 94549
Telephone 510-299-8080 Ext #228